Snowed

Snowed

Snowed: *to have been deceived, persuaded, or charmed glibly*

VIRGINIA BENNETT

SNOWED
By Virginia Bennett
© 2021 Virginia Bennett

First Paperback Edition
Produced by Raab & Co. | raabandco.com
Cover by Andrew Bell | andrewbelldesigns.com

ISBN: 978-1-7947-8374-4

Contents

1

Forecast

"How does this look?" I asked my office assistant, LeeAnn, as I walked into the kitchen. I was getting ready for a blind date, and was aiming for that classic, effortless look that really isn't all that effortless. After trying on four different outfits, I had settled on a black cashmere sweater with ivory wool slacks, sling-back heels, and a Swarovski crystal necklace. Finally, I felt comfortable.

"Why aren't you wearing a skirt or a dress?" LeeAnn asked, as she did paperwork at my kitchen table. "You have such nice legs. Why don't you flaunt them?"

"Thank you," I said. "I did wear a skirt on my last blind date, but the guy wouldn't stop looking at my legs. He called himself a 'leg aficionado.' So, for this guy tonight, I'm nixing the bare legs and wearing slacks. I'd like to meet someone who's interested in what's on the inside first, and then, if we go out again, I'll bring out the legs."

I grabbed a bottle of Provenance Estate Cab and two bags

of my chocolate-covered almonds that I was selling at upscale grocery stores in San Francisco. I'd grown up on an almond farm in California, and had recently started a line of gourmet nuts. As I tied ribbon around the bags, LeeAnn looked up and asked, "Why are you taking those?"

"It's his birthday," I said.

"His birthday? Where are his friends?" LeeAnn asked. "You know, his buddies, his family? Why isn't he doing something with them? No offense, but he's never even met you. What's his name, anyways?"

"Liam O'Connor," I said. "He lives in Alamo. Here's his phone number. There was something about his voice on the phone that I liked. I felt as though I'd heard it before. Besides," I added, thinking about my own family, "I'm an only child, and if it weren't for my kids, I might be home alone on my birthday, too."

Earlier in the day, Liam had called and asked if I didn't mind if he wore jeans. I told him he could probably wear anything he wanted, except for maybe his birthday suit. He laughed and confirmed the details: 7:00 p.m. at Il Postino, a local Italian restaurant. I had been there many times before, and it was one of my favorites. The food was delicious, and the whimsical building, with turrets and ivy climbing on the walls outside, evoked a Disney fairy tale.

After LeeAnn left, my daughter, Hannah, called to say she needed a ride home from soccer practice. She couldn't get her dad on the phone, and all of her friends had left the field. I figured he was out on the golf course again. I told her I'd be right there. By the time I drove to pick her up at the soccer field, then dropped her off at my former husband Dale's house, it put me half an hour behind schedule.

Pulling up to the restaurant, I parked on the street, since the valet had a long line of cars waiting, and hurried inside. I went straight to the cocktail lounge and walked along the thirty-foot coppertop bar lined with glass candle votives. Wondering if he was still there, I hesitantly made my way down the crowded bar, looking for a guy who could be him. When I reached the end, I turned around and saw a tall, strikingly handsome man stand up from a barstool. As he stood, I noticed that he kept his body at an angle from mine, not directly meeting me straight on. He tilted his head just a bit, and, looking over in my direction, gave me a big, friendly smile.

Relieved that he was still there, I smiled back and walked toward him at the end of the bar. "I'm so glad you didn't leave," I said. "I'm sorry I'm late. I tried calling to let you know. I had to run and pick up my daughter from soccer practice."

"I usually would have left after fifteen minutes," he said, still smiling. "But you sounded so nice on the phone that I decided to wait a while longer."

Liam was tall, with broad shoulders and a slim waist, and yet he looked slightly husky, like a bodyguard. He had a natural stature, the kind that turns heads. Funnily enough, though, I had walked right past him at the beginning of the bar. He had been sitting on a barstool, talking to a female bartender.

The host escorted us to a table that Liam had reserved in the Atrium Alcove, a semi-private space within the main dining room. The exposed brick walls and fireplaces made it feel warm and intimate. As I set the bottle of wine and the two bags of chocolate-covered almonds on the table, I turned to Liam and said, "Happy birthday! These are for you."

"Thanks," he said. "I can't wait to try them."

The waiter stopped by to ask if we wanted something to drink.

I looked over at Liam to see what he was drinking, and

noticed he had a glass of white wine, which was about a quarter full.

"Sure," I said to the waiter. "I'll have some white wine. Liam, what are you having?"

"How about the Rombauer?" he said.

"Sounds great."

Liam ordered half a bottle. *Half a bottle?* I thought. Oh, well, that's okay. I certainly didn't need more than one glass, anyway. Besides, since I was late and had missed the cocktail happy-half-hour, there went the before-dinner drink, which was perfectly fine. But I wondered if Liam had ordered only half a bottle to save money, or because he'd already had a drink while he was waiting for me, or if he was being conscientious and didn't want to be wasteful.

He had a great smile and loose, light brown curls that were perfectly disheveled, as if they had come straight out of *GQ* magazine. He had bright blue eyes, a smooth complexion, and straight white teeth. Why did he look so familiar? I wondered. Then it dawned on me: he looked like the star of the TV show *Here Come the Brides*, Robert Brown, whom I'd had a crush on as a teenager.

After the waiter left, I noticed that Liam had taken his napkin and placed it neatly on his lap. He rested his forearms on the table and leaned in toward me, making me feel like I was the only person in the room. I'd been so used to Dale taking pride in his ability to listen to two conversations at once that I appreciated Liam's interest in what I had to say. After talking about our respective days, I asked him about his children.

"Three are married, and one is about to go on a mission," he said. "They're all grown and independent, living in other states."

"Oh," I said. "What kind of mission?"

"A Mormon mission," he said. "How about you? How many kids do you have?"

"I have two," I said. "They're much younger than yours. Eight and ten. I was married to their dad for thirteen years, and we divorced three years ago. How long were you married?"

"What are you having for dinner?" Liam answered.

I thought he must not have heard me, so I asked again: "How long were you married?"

"Let's not talk about that right now," he replied.

There was a split-second of awkwardness before I thought, *Either that's strange, or this isn't the time to delve into those details.* Better to keep the conversation light. But then again, it was just a normal question, right? Was he hiding something? Or maybe I was too nosy too fast. Curiosity killed the cat, as the saying goes, and if that was true, then I'd used up my nine lives a long time ago.

Over dinner, I told Liam about my family's orchards, and how in addition to marketing and selling our almonds to grocery stores, I had also established an account with a top restaurant in San Francisco. "Interesting your family is in agriculture," he said, "because I grew up on a farm in Illinois."

"You know," I said, "you're the first person I've met in thirteen years of living in the Bay Area who shares a background in farming."

Toward the end of dinner, Liam asked the waiter to bring a dish for the chocolate-covered almonds I'd given him. He poured a few out onto the dish, tasted a couple, and liked them so much that he motioned for the waiter to come over to our table. "You ought to take some of these to the chef," he said. "They're served at one of the top restaurants in San Francisco. The chef might want to know what the competition is serving."

The waiter nodded and took some on a small plate into the kitchen before he returned with the chef's business card.

Leaving the restaurant, Liam and I walked side by side to my car. I noticed that he was wearing jeans and nice leather oxford shoes. I liked his casual style. As we looked up at the clear night sky, I motioned to where my car was parked in front of the restaurant. It had been my seventy-three-year-old mom's car, a silver Lexus SUV, but because of her advancing Alzheimer's disease, she could no longer drive. My parents were pleased that, having recently sold my own car, I was now driving hers. Plus, given my sadness over my mom's rapidly deteriorating condition, driving her car made me feel close to her.

Liam opened the car door, thanked me for the birthday treats, and shut the door without so much as a kiss or a hug. It was a busy street, and maybe he wanted to get back onto the sidewalk as quickly as possible, I thought. Or maybe he was a proper gentleman. Either way, he exuded poise and a low-key self-assuredness.

When I got back to my house, I opened up my computer and sent Liam an email. "I had such a nice time," I wrote. "Thanks for including me in your birthday celebration." About twenty minutes later, he sent me an e-card. It was an animated musical e-card with a cartoon of a boy and a girl sitting on a curved yellow moon, holding hands and singing, with their feet dangling over the Earth. Behind them was a canopy of big, bright white stars set against a midnight blue sky. Liam had written, "Thank you again for the birthday treats and your company at dinner." The card was peppy, catchy, and creative, and the fact that he would send such a sweet and romantic thank-you set him apart.

The next morning, Liam called at nine. I was in the other room, and when I noticed I had missed his call, half an hour had already passed. I tried calling him back, but there was no answer. Over the next day or two, he called a couple more times. Each time he called, I found myself wanting to talk to him longer. I couldn't figure out where I'd heard his voice before, but it sounded so familiar.

Liam was a regional sales manager for a tech company, and he traveled a lot for work. Here and there he would send emails. In one, he explained at great length about a genetic disease he carried called hemochromatosis, or iron overload, which he related to his Viking ancestry. In another, he asked me to describe myself eating a peach. Now, if Liam had asked me to describe myself putting on lingerie that would have ended it for me, but to describe myself eating a peach, now that got my attention. Right away, I thought about all those summers on the farm when I would stand at the kitchen counter, leaning over the sink, eating a peach and slurping the juice as it dripped off my hands and ran down my wrists.

A farmer named Ernie, who was a close family friend, grew the most delicious peaches I have ever eaten to this day. He picked them plump and ripe, just at the point that their sweet smell was as enticing as their taste. A few weeks before Liam asked me to describe myself eating a peach, Ernie had told me about a book called *Four Seasons in Five Senses*, which, in a serendipitous coincidence, was all about peaches. It just so happened that it was my month to choose the book for my local book group, and that's the one I'd chosen.

Written by David Masumoto, the book compares peach farming to an orchestra with each instrument playing its part. A second-generation peach farmer, Masumoto also details the decline of farming in America, noting that "In 1900, one out of ten Americans operated a farm; by 1997, it was less than one in a hundred." Each chapter in the book is named for one of the senses, with the fourth being "The Art of Taste." So, when I emailed Liam back, I told him about the book, and suggested that he turn to page 122. "How to eat a peach begins with first finding the perfect peach," Masumoto writes, before going on to describe the red, velvety-soft, voluptuous ones. His prized peach was the Sun Crest, which of all the varieties, was also my favorite.

I knew this probably wasn't what Liam was looking for, and yet he replied respectfully, saying he was going to purchase the book and read it. And he did. What I didn't realize at the time was that the book and our discussions about it marked the first of many things that would set in motion what later became our motto: "Let's Go Farming."

2

Inclement

Growing up in the country without any siblings, I spent a lot of time alone. My dad, Sam Bennett, was always working on our family farm, so dinnertime was no different from any other time of the day. He would be gone all day, and many nights, too, irrigating or harvesting the fields, while my mom, Irene, worked full-time as a legal secretary. My grandpa Fred, my dad's dad, was my babysitter. He picked me up from school every day in his 1965 Dodge pickup truck, the kind with a push-button shift. While my classmates were at soccer practice, I was out in the fields with my dad and grandpa, watching while they burned wheat stubble and harvested corn with big giant combines. One time, they built a bridge over a canal on our property, and my dad carved my initials with the date in the cement.

I had a wire-haired terrier named Tammy, who looked like a little wind-up toy. I'd put her in my red wooden wagon, a Radio Flyer with removable sides, along with my dinner, and pull it out to the orchard. My mom would cook hamburger patties that I'd eat and share with Tammy. As much as I loved having dinner with my dog, I longed for brothers and sisters. Our neighbors were a family of eight, and playing with them gave me an experience of the fullness of life that having siblings could bring. As I got older, I understood how I might have benefited from having siblings, whether it was learning how to assert myself, or having to negotiate for what I needed.

When my first husband, Dale, and I got married, we talked about having children. He had one older brother, and wanted two kids. I wanted four. At the time, I thought the subject was still open for discussion, and didn't worry too much about it. But down the line, it proved to be more of an issue than I had anticipated.

I'd met Dale in California, a few years after graduating from college in Washington State. He was confident, athletic, and well-educated, and, like me, his family had a long legacy in California. I was attracted to his passionate personality and ambitious nature; whatever Dale was doing, he did it big. He had a quick wit and a contagious laugh, but just as quick as he could smile and ad-lib one-liners, he could also turn it on its head and ask me questions with double negatives that often stymied me. He sounded like a litigator.

Within a year of dating, we were married. I was twenty-seven, and while I had some hesitations, I felt like it was time to get married. "I'm going to make you the best husband ever," Dale told me. We soon had two healthy, beautiful children, Cody and Hannah, whom I adored, and I hoped to have more. But one afternoon, after nine years of marriage, Dale announced that he'd had a vasectomy. He came home and plopped himself down on the sofa with a bag of frozen peas. Any chance of us having more children had been decided by him, and him alone. His unilateral decision was such a betrayal that I couldn't get past it for years to come.

In the years that followed, I begged Dale to go to marriage counseling. I had begun to feel like the light in my soul was slowly being extinguished. Dale was adamant about not going, and, in what seemed to be a prevailing theme in our marriage, it was his way or the highway. No matter how hard I tried to engage in thoughtful communication with him, Dale would stonewall and run right over the top of me. If I told him that the way he spoke to me was hurtful, he'd tell me I was overly sensitive. He would forget numerous conversations we'd had, where I thought we were both present, right there in the moment, acknowledging what the other was saying. But later he would tell me he didn't remember the conversation. "I forgot," he routinely said, so I went to counseling by myself. I thought that maybe when he saw me going, he would change his mind and we could go together. But it never worked out that way. In fact, one time, after I had been going to counseling for a while, he asked, "So how's that workin' for you?" I didn't even know how to answer, because his tone was so condescending.

Then there was the document ambush. About six months before we divorced, Dale rushed into the kitchen and demanded that I sign a legal document. "What is this?" I asked. He became incensed, as if my question about the content were actually questioning his authority. "It has to do with the properties."

"You want me to sign this right now?" I asked.

"Yes, it's for an important meeting that I'm on my way to. Sign it now," he said, holding out a pen in front of me. As I took the pen from his hand, I didn't know what to say. I could tell from his indignant attitude that I wasn't going to get any more details, and so, without asking another question, I signed the document and asked him for a copy.

Once I finally got a copy, after asking numerous times, I took it to a real estate lawyer to find out what I had signed. I couldn't decipher the legal jargon, and I also wanted to know if a person could make another person sign a document without having them read it first. The lawyer told me that the document skipped me in Dale's family's estate planning. Furthermore, it stipulated that in the event of a legal termination of marriage, all of his properties and their proceeds would go to him. I was hurt not because I was excluded, but by the fact that Dale would have me sign a legal document that affected me without first explaining what it was. Did he think I was so dumb that I wouldn't understand, I wondered, or did he not value my input?

As for my question about signing a document without being allowed to read it first, the lawyer said that a contract signed under duress is considered illegal. "In this case," he said, "it could be considered psychological pressure. It makes one wonder about your spouse's intentions." The lawyer also told me of a good divorce attorney he knew; he didn't push it, but he did write down his name and phone number. "Just in case," he said as he handed me the contact information.

I somberly left the attorney's office and, for the first time, considered the possibility of ending my marriage.

At my next solo appointment with the marriage counselor, I told her what had happened. Her response surprised me. She used the strongest language I'd heard her use in the entire year we'd been working together. "Well," she said, "I have thought that your husband has been emotionally and verbally abusive." *Why in the world hasn't she told me this before?* I thought. *I've been going to her for almost a year, and now she tells me this?* After thinking about it, though, it did make sense, because

I had been having anxiety attacks. It felt like I had an anvil on my chest, and I couldn't breathe. When I'd go running with my girlfriends, I would have to stop every few minutes or so because it felt like I wasn't getting enough oxygen. I went to the doctor and found out that my blood pressure, which was normally very low, was now very high. I felt like I was drowning, and divorce was my only life preserver, as if our marriage were a sinking ship. The only way to survive was to get off somehow, or go down with the ship. If our marriage was an airplane in free fall, then I had to put on my own oxygen mask first.

Eventually, after thirteen years, I felt so emotionally worn down that I filed for divorce. In the weeks leading up to my filing, Dale kept trying to stall me. One week, he said, "Don't file tomorrow, it's my mom's mah-jongg group on Wednesday, and it'll be in the local paper," and another week it was, "Don't file now, it's my dad's Elks Club meeting, and it'll be in the paper." It wasn't until the eleventh hour (or more like the *twelfth*), after he'd run out of excuses, that Dale finally said he would go to marriage counseling, after all. But by that time, I had become stubborn, and my situation felt hopeless. I felt that if Dale had cared enough about our relationship to make it work, he would have gone with me before we'd reached this point.

But even though I'd filed for divorce, I felt disloyal to Dale and to my children for doing so. I don't like to go against my word, and as traditional marriage vows state: Till death do us part. When I say, "I love you," I love deeply, and my love doesn't stop on a dime.

Moreover, with the divorce came a custody arrangement for the children. It was a forced, premature emptying of the nest that I was not ready for, nor could I have been prepared for the feeling of no longer being needed. I missed hugging and holding my children beyond belief, and I missed the nighttime rituals of reading books and saying prayers. When the children were not with me, I felt like I was losing them. I also feared for their safety when they were with their father, and would have gut-wrenching anxiety attacks in the middle of the night.

I mourned the death of our marriage like it was the death of a person, the death of an entity. There was the loss of him. The loss of me. The loss of him and me together.

Ever since I was seven, when my grandmother started taking me to church with her, I have had a deep and personal relationship with God. When I was ten, my dad, who grew up Southern Baptist, enrolled me in a Catholic school. Church has always been my sanctuary and place of refuge. For Dale, however, church did not have the same meaning. When we were dating, I mistakenly assumed that because of Dale's conservative background, we shared the same morals and religious perspective. But, in fact, after our kids were baptized, Dale started refusing to go to church on a regular basis. He said he'd stopped going at five years old, and that religion was a crutch for weak people who couldn't think for themselves. But even if he didn't want to go to church, I still wanted our kids to come with me. However, it was hard to get an eight-year-old boy to church on a Sunday when his dad was leaving at the same time to go hit golf balls, or lounging on the sofa in his sweatpants, eating ice cream and watching TV.

For the first few months after the divorce, I attended Sunday mass seeking peace and comfort. It was the same church where my kids had been baptized and where we would go as a family. One Sunday after the divorce, I found myself sitting in the pew behind the Wellingtons, a family that had lived close to ours. Mr. Wellington played poker with Dale, and Mrs. Wellington and I had been swim team moms together. Sitting there, staring at their family unit only brought home the fact that I was no longer part of one. I could not stop the tears from running down my cheeks and dripping off my chin. The priest stopped mid-sentence in his homily and looked over at me, which made my face feel like it was burning up. Embarrassed, I looked down and dug into my purse for Kleenex. After mass, some churchgoers came over and offered comforting, compassionate words, not knowing at all what my problem was, while others, it seemed, steered clear.

Within a month and a half of my having filed for divorce, Dale began dating another mom at our kids' school. It made me feel expendable that he could move on so quickly. He ended up marrying this same woman a year and a half later, whereas it took me well over two years just to stop grieving. My way of life as I knew it—being together in a family unit, that is—no longer existed. In Orinda, the conservative bedroom community where we lived, news of a divorce spread like wildfire and carried with it a social stigma. One time, while I was grocery shopping, a swim team mom rounded the corner as I was pushing my cart to the end of the detergent aisle. She looked at me, then quickly backed up—literally into someone behind her—and off she went around an end cap display of fancy vinegars.

3

Balmy

When I was finally ready to start dating again, friends would set me up with different guys. There always seemed to be some guy who was a friend of a friend, divorced, widowed, separated, or still married and soon to be divorcing (no, thank you). When nothing clicked, my running and hiking partner, Sophia, convinced me to sign up for an online dating service. I was dubious at first, but Sophia insisted that this was the only way I'd meet someone.

After I got over my nerves, the process of creating a profile for myself, then clicking on someone I might want to date, felt daring—like we were a bunch of aging high school rebels out on the prowl. But it also felt impersonal; I preferred the old-fashioned way of dating.

Once I'd finally figured out how to maneuver my way through the matchmaking website, I started dating up a storm. After dropping the kids off at school, I would go for a coffee date at 8:00 a.m., then I would drive to Patterson to do the bookkeeping, manage the office for our farm, and take care of my mom, before it was time for a lunch date, followed by an after-work drink at Pier 39 in San Francisco. I drove up and down highways 680, 580, 80, and 99 to dinners, lunches, and movies, with an anesthesiologist, a raisin farmer, a PGA golfer, a contractor, an actor on the TV show *CSI*, a plumber, an investment banker, and the sole owner of an island. My dates ran the gamut.

When the twentieth date came, that was my limit. I had gone on nineteen dates in the course of six months, and I had little desire or ability to give my dating life any more time or energy. But then I saw Liam's picture. I hadn't seen it until I'd narrowed the search to six feet tall with blue eyes. It wasn't a close-up photo. He was relaxing on a boat, nicely dressed, with the sun setting in the background. Intriguing.

After my first date with Liam, yes, we had the occasional emails and phone calls back and forth, but those eventually dwindled down such that we had no contact for about two months. I was so busy with my mom and the kids, and also the nuts, that I didn't think too much about it. Though I did wonder what had happened to him. I figured he'd probably found someone else.

Nevertheless, in late June, when the Sun Crest peaches were ripe, I sent Liam an email. "Dear Liam," I wrote. "I don't know if you are around, or if you have found someone else, but either way, I have some of those Sun Crest peaches, and I wondered if you'd like to try some." He emailed me right back. He wrote that he was at a convention, but would very much like to try them, and he would call me when he got back into town.

A few days later, Liam called. "Hey, how about those

peaches," he said. "Still got any?"

"Sure do!" I said. "I'll have some on Wednesday. Maybe we could meet somewhere in Alamo, since I'll be driving right through there."

My kids had a swim meet nearby in Moraga, and I'd planned to go watch them.

"Yeah, give me a call," he said. "I don't know my schedule, but we can talk that day and figure it out."

That Tuesday, I drove out to my parents' farm in Patterson and stayed in the guesthouse, which we'd nicknamed the "little house," as it was next to my mom and dad's house, which we called the "big house." I planned to drive out to Ernie's peach ranch the following day. He picked them fresh and perfectly ripe every morning at 4:00 a.m., and opened his gate to the public at 7:30. Some days he sold out in forty-five minutes, other days a bit longer, but you never knew, so if you wanted a box of Ernie's delicious peaches, you had to hustle and get out to his ranch before they were gone.

Wednesday morning, I woke up at 6:00 a.m. It takes about twenty-five minutes to drive to Ernie's from the little house, and I wanted to get there early. But eager as I was to buy some of his fresh peaches, I didn't feel that great. During the night, my Cairn terrier, Gus, had started barking and growling underneath my bed. It woke me up. Then about an hour later, I sat right up in bed and broke out in a cold sweat, feeling sick and very strange. I lay back down, but I tossed and turned, dozing on and off until it was time to get up.

It was an effort just to get dressed. I was really dragging. I drove out to Ernie's, bought a couple boxes of peaches, and drove straight back to the little house. After I unloaded the boxes, I went into the big house and checked on my mom. I helped her with some things in the kitchen, before driving her into town for her hair appointment at 10:30. Because of her

Alzheimer's, I always stayed the hour and fifteen minutes it took for her cut and color.

While I was waiting, Liam called. We arranged to meet that afternoon in the parking lot of Read Booksellers, in the Blackhawk shopping plaza in Alamo. My mom and I got back to the big house about noon, and I prepared lunch for my parents. After our meal, I tried to work in the farm office in the big house, but I gave up after a while and went back to the little house. I sank down onto the sofa.

I kept watching the clock. It was so hard to get up and shower and get dressed, but I didn't want to miss the opportunity to see Liam. As I was putting on my makeup, I noticed a big red bump on my left temple, right between my eye and my hairline. I must have been bitten by something, I thought, and that was probably why I didn't feel well. I finished doing my hair and forced myself to get dressed.

A few weeks earlier, I had taken my mom shopping, and along with buying clothes for her, I'd also bought myself a short skirt in a pinkish peach color with a tiny floral pattern. It was not a miniskirt, but it was high enough above the knee to get the picture; it was time to bring out the legs. I wore the skirt with a cardigan sweater and a sleeveless blouse. The sweater was for the cold, foggy swim meet evenings so close to the Bay, and the sleeveless blouse underneath was for the hot Central Valley.

I was ready to go. I put the peaches back into my SUV, went over to say goodbye to my mom, and left to meet Liam. Some forty-five minutes later, as I was pulling into the busy shopping area, I spotted him from a distance. He was standing next to his car, smiling in his white linen shirt, khaki shorts, and leather flip-flops, looking like a star athlete. I got out of my car and waved. I felt a little nervous. When I opened up the back I could sense Liam walking up to me. Trying to keep my nerves under control, I kept telling myself, *This is just two people sharing something good to eat.*

I pretended to arrange the already arranged peaches in the flat.

"Those are some nice peaches," Liam said. "Can't wait to try them. Hey, you want to join me for a burger over at Alamo Grill?" It was right across the parking lot.

"I would have liked to," I said, "but I'm on the way to my kids' swim meet in Moraga."

"Okay, have fun, and hey," he said, pausing for emphasis, "thanks for the peaches!"

And that was it. I slowly got into my car, pulled out, and watched Liam put the peaches in his trunk. When he started to look over, I looked away. But as I drove past him crossing the street to the Alamo Grill, we both caught each other's eye and smiled.

I drove another forty-five minutes to Moraga. Between the billowing fog, which made it feel like it was freezing cold, and the fact that I felt so crummy, I could only watch Cody and Hannah swim one race each. I had to tell them how sorry I was that I had to go, but I wasn't feeling well.

"I'll see you on Friday," I told my kids. I was taking them to a ranch in Colorado, and we were leaving that weekend.

By Friday, the red bump I had noticed near my eye was the size of a goose egg. It was sticking straight out, perpendicular from my temple. I looked scary, like I was wearing a mask on Halloween. That morning I took Hannah with me to the hospital, where they said they could give me a cortisone shot to reduce its size, but that I would have to wait a couple of hours. Forget it, I thought. I didn't have time.

The day before, I had called the pest control guy, and he'd

come out earlier that morning. He'd pointed out that above my bed was a huge black widow spiderweb. There was another one within the lace curtains in the bathroom. He said the black widow was probably on its way to the bathroom to get water during the night, and that the dog had startled it, or the spider had startled the dog, thus the barking, and it had crawled up over the bed, and over me. Maybe I had moved when I heard the dog bark, and the spider had bitten me. It was too late to get an antivenom shot since it had to be administered within the first twenty-four hours in order to be effective.

The Sunday after being bitten by the black widow, Cody, Hannah, and I left for our vacation at the Sylvan Dale Guest Ranch in Loveland, Colorado. When my kids and I arrived, we met up with some family friends who had told us about the ranch; we had scheduled to be there at the same time. The family had two boys, one Cody's age, and one about Hannah's age. The dad, Dr. Mark Roberts, was the director of a large metropolitan hospital. His wife, Deborah, was a nurse.

I called out to Deborah when I saw her, "Hi there! It's so good to see you. This place is absolutely beautiful."

"We are so glad you made it," she said. "You and the kids are going to love it here. The people are so nice, and the horses are easy to ride. The overnight cattle drive is an experience you'll never forget—oh, my goodness, are you okay? That lump, right by your eye, what is that? It looks like it might block some of your vision. Can you see alright?"

Knowing she was a nurse, I didn't mind too much that she'd asked me about it, although I did find the lump pretty embarrassing. No matter how many times I tried to pull my hair over it, it wouldn't stay, because it stuck out too far.

"I was bitten by a black widow," I said.

Deborah didn't make a comment, but quickly called her husband over. "Mark, come take a look at this."

Oh, brother, I thought. *This is like show-and-tell.*

Dr. Roberts came over, and he and Deborah both tilted their heads from one side to the other, examining the bite, oohing and aahing while they gaped at me. "Isn't that something," they said, nodding at each other. "Her body is isolating it."

"What does that mean?"

"Your body has sealed off the venom's neurotoxin into one area as a way to protect itself," Deborah explained.

The funny thing was, I'd always had a weird feeling about black widows. As a child, I had to work around them on the farm, and they gave me the willies. One summer, when I was about eleven or twelve years old, one of my chores out in the orchards was to tear milk carton boxes off the almond tree yearlings. Open-ended on both sides, the milk carton boxes were dropped by hand over the baby trees after planting, and the cartons rested on the ground. The carton protected the yearling bark from weed spray, rodents, and sunburn. When it came time to remove the boxes, the trees had grown some and leafed out a bit, so I could no longer pull them up and off the same way they had been put on. Instead, the boxes had to be torn off. To my horror, I saw numerous black widow spiders and egg sacs. About three quarters of the milk carton boxes were filled with the messy, unorganized, sticky webs that crackle when pulled apart and are distinctive to the poisonous spiders.

The very first boxes that I pulled off creeped me out. I quickly got some thick gloves and squashed the black widows; if I squashed an egg sac, hundreds of tiny baby spiders, invisible to the human eye, would scramble in every direction. I did this for the first few boxes or so and felt revulsion every time. After that, even though the spiders creeped me out, I just ripped off the cartons and let them be.

In spite of my embarrassing spider bite, the kids and I had

a great time in Colorado. The Sylvan Dale Guest Ranch was a spectacular place. The Big Thompson River, which ran right through it, was lined with quaking aspen and cottonwood trees, and here and there open meadows spread out in front of majestic rock mountains. The kids and I stayed for one week in a guest cottage near the main lodge, which had a meeting place, a recreation center for square dancing, a library, horse-shoe games, a swimming pool, and a bear trap, cage and all. I was glad a bear was caught on the last night we were there, and not the first.

One afternoon we went river rafting, and one night we went on an overnight cattle drive up in the high country. The lodge had neither television nor cell reception, so if you wanted contact with the outside world, you had to use a pay phone in the lodge. Each day I would check my messages and call my dad to see how my mom was doing. I was excited when, out of the blue, I got a message from Liam. "Hey, Virginia, just calling to say hello. I'm driving to one of my accounts. Hope you're having a great day. Bye."

I stood straight up when I heard Liam's mellifluous voice.

"What's wrong?" Cody asked. "Who is it? What's the matter?"

"Oh, it's nothing," I said. "Everything's okay."

4

Clement

When the kids and I got back from our trip to Colorado, the black widow bite was still a visible bump. It was now two weeks later, and it had gone down only a little bit. I was excited to call Liam and tell him I was back, and to let him know that I had received his message. Never did I think he would say, "Would you like to go out to dinner?"

I was staying at my parents' guesthouse in Patterson with my kids the week before their swim meets resumed. Since Alamo was only about forty-five minutes away from Patterson, I asked Liam if he would like to come join us for dinner. Because of my mom's Alzheimer's, I didn't have much one-on-one time with my kids anymore, and I didn't want to lose the limited time I did have with them.

I couldn't believe how well our time together went. Liam was gracious about my spider bite, and didn't say a word until I mentioned it. The kids played basketball with Liam, and then my parents walked over from the big house to say hello.

After they left, we sat down for dinner, and Cody said the blessing. Back then, I was able to take Cody to church with me, and it was noticeable how well he absorbed the lessons and homilies. Whenever he said grace before a meal, or prayed out loud, he relayed a spirituality beyond his years.

My second date-date with Liam occurred last minute. I was driving to Patterson for the weekend to help care for my mom, as well as do the usual bookkeeping and payroll for the farm. Because of my mom's deteriorating condition, she could no longer manage their finances. My dad had asked me to step in and manage them in her place.

Driving down 680, I called Liam to say that I was on my way to Patterson. He'd often ask me to call him if I was heading in that direction, so we could meet for a bite to eat. So that's what I did, and we made plans to meet for dinner at a local restaurant called Bridges in Alamo.

When I arrived at the restaurant, Liam wasn't there yet. I had never been to Bridges, so I thought I would wait outside on a wrought iron bench by the front door. I was surprised that I had to wait for about twenty minutes; usually I was the one who was late.

"Hey, why are you sitting outside?" Liam asked, as he walked up to the restaurant. "You didn't go in?" He said it with a smile and a polite, easygoing manner that put me at ease.

Bridges was a dark, woodsy-feeling place with two TV screens over the bar; a crowd of young professional singles mingled about the noisy restaurant, sipping drinks. We put our name down for dinner, then walked over to a high cocktail table and waited there. After we had each ordered a glass of white wine, Liam immediately started talking about his previous marriages in great detail. He seemed to have been saving up the answer to the question I had asked him on our first date in Orinda.

Unprompted, he proceeded to tell me that he had been married three times. When he talked about his children, he talked about their mom, just as he had before, but now it was in the context of her having been his first wife. I sat there looking at him, thinking, *Should this be something to think twice about?* But then I thought, *Once a person gets married and divorced, it changes everything.* By this time, Dale was already on his second marriage, and from what he'd told me recently, it was already on the rocks. So even though out of all my girlfriends, only one had been divorced, I could see how someone could end up in more than one marriage.

As Liam sipped his glass of wine, he told me that he'd been a virgin when he got married. He'd been brought up Mormon, and it made me happy that he had such a spiritually minded upbringing. He said that he did not believe in sex outside of marriage, nor did he want to be used by women. Here was a man with scruples, I thought.

When our table was ready, the cocktail waitress escorted us to a large, half-circle booth. We scooted in so there were about twenty inches between us. Liam ordered an appetizer of sautéed mushrooms with red wine and shallots, a salad to share, and we each ordered steak and potatoes. We sipped on wine and talked. It was satisfying to speak and feel heard, and to be listened to so attentively by a man who seemed so understanding.

While I was talking, the sautéed mushrooms arrived. Liam proceeded to pick up the au gratin dish of mushrooms and serve us both on two small plates that he'd asked for when he'd ordered them. What I didn't notice was that as he was reaching for the mushrooms, and serving them on the plates, he was simultaneously inching a little closer to me with each reach.

As Liam finished serving and put the plates down, he was,

without my having noticed, sitting right next to me. He leaned over, and then ever so gently brushed his cheek against mine. I instantly felt a current of electricity so strong that it caught me off guard.

"Did you feel that?" I said. "I mean, did you feel what I just felt?" I stopped talking. At that point, I knew I couldn't retract what I had just said. Liam looked at me, smiled, and gradually mouthed the word, "Whaaat?"

The rest of the dinner was a hazy blur. I was aware of my surroundings, but I couldn't hear a thing except for what Liam was saying.

After dinner, he invited me over to see his place, which was only five minutes away. "I'll take a quick look," I said, and we drove over to his house. Afterward, as I stepped toward my car to leave, all of a sudden Liam picked me up and swung me around in the air. "Oh, no, put me down," I said, giggling. The action of our bodies touching closely sparked the embers of my heart.

On the days when I was in Patterson, in addition to doing the bookkeeping in the office, I would also join my dad as he did the field checks. As we drove the dirt roads that separated the almond orchards, I would write down anything and everything that had occurred during that day or week. I recorded my father's challenges, his meetings with employees, buyers, equipment companies, water districts, and anything else that arose. I called this log my "Almond Timeline." I had learned about how to keep track of things this way when I'd worked in sales at Clorox.

In farming, there are particular tasks that are done according to the season and the weather. A certain method or procedure done in January, or in June, can be done in a similar way the following year around the same time—and the next year, and the next, and the next after that for the same commodity. Each year, of course, there can be an anomaly, but for the most part there are standard orchard tasks. I kept all of this information in my Almond Timeline, which felt personal to me, almost like a diary.

Some days, my dad would share stories with me from years past, and I'd get to hear about how his dad, uncle, or grandpa had saved the day. One year, the lima beans were in a windrow, waiting to be threshed, when a big rain came, the pods burst open, and the entire crop was destroyed. That particular year, when my dad wasn't in school, he had worked hoeing weeds from sunup to sundown, and they had to plow it all under.

My dad was devastated, and his uncle Maynard told him, "Next year, we'll just have to plant the seed a little deeper."

Yes, deeper, but the deeper meaning was that you can't change what happened; all you can do is try to do better the next year. Optimism prevails. That is farming: faith in the next crop.

After my second date with Liam, I was excited to tell my dad a little bit more about him. It was all business when my dad and I were out in the pickup, checking on the trees and monitoring various projects, so I rarely brought up personal matters. No errant conversations. Now and then there would be a lull, and on one particular day, during one such lull, I broke the business rule. I had not talked about anyone I'd dated since my divorce, except for the raisin farmer in Fresno who spoke continuously about helicopter skiing with tech company giants.

Driving through one of the orchards, I told my dad how Liam had grown up on a farm in the Midwest, where he would do chores early in the morning, and then attend Mormon religious classes, all before going to school. My dad valued a strong work ethic, so I expected him to be interested, but he made no comment and instead started talking about water issues on the farm.

It was a challenge having my dad as my manager, and our family business as my employer. Because I was talking to my dad, it was sometimes a stretch for me to figure out if it was the subject matter he wasn't interested in, or the fact that it didn't concern the farm. Either way, he didn't like to chitchat. He taught me to stay focused and, as he often said to me, "Keep your nose to the grindstone." My dad, a tall, handsome man who stood six-foot-five, took that motto seriously. Don't look up or pause until the race is over, and you will reap the rewards was the lesson he taught me from a young age.

Needless to say, my attempt to bring Liam into the conversation fell flat, but as I would later come to realize, my dad had heard every word I said.

5

Heat Wave

Not long after my second date with Liam, I went on a girls' getaway trip with some old friends from college. Eight of us met up in Seattle and drove to our friend Sarah's vacation house, which overlooked a golf course in Tacoma.

One day we went hiking, and on the day we were supposed to leave, my friend Melinda and I went out for a morning run. In college, Melinda and I had gone running together almost every day at 6:00 a.m. She slept in the bunk bed beside mine and had an internal alarm clock like no other. Without fail, she would wake me up for our early morning runs. It was now twenty-one years later, and whenever we were together, Melinda would still wake me up to hit the pavement or the trails. I tend to be slow out of the gate, but I always pick up speed, and a good strong cup of coffee is a sure fix for my super low blood pressure.

"Where do you want to go?" Melinda asked.

"Anywhere out here is good."

"Well, do you want to go over by the clubhouse and then to the left, or to the right and around?"

"I guess we could go to the right and come back around."

It was not unusual for us to banter a bit back and forth until we each felt satisfied that the other was comfortable with where we were going to run. We not only ran together in college but also ran daily together for a couple more years after we'd graduated and entered the working world.

So off we went, zigzagging through orange construction cones, both on and off the pavement. We talked about our moms, but it wasn't long before she asked about Liam.

"Liam is really different than any other guy I've ever met," I told her. "He was raised on a farm in Illinois and has a great work ethic. During college, he won the Illinois State wrestling championship."

"Well, we'll have to meet him," Melinda said. "Let's all get together some time. That's a good way to see how he is with your friends."

"You're right," I said. "Tonight, when I get back, Liam said to call him. We're going out to dinner. I'm so excited, but also a little nervous."

We had ended up running much further than we had planned so that by the time we got back to the house, we were not only sweaty but also grimy from all the dirt in the air caused by the construction at the golf course around Sarah's house. I couldn't wait to jump in the shower. We took off our shoes in the mudroom and walked into the kitchen, where we found a contractor and a lot of commotion. It turned out that with all the work they had been doing, a sewer line had broken and flooded Sarah's basement. As a result, the water was turned off for the moment, and there would be no hot water for a while.

I didn't care. I just wanted to be clean for my date with Liam.

As soon as the water came back on, I jumped in the shower. It was so cold that I nicked my legs a few times trying to shave them. Never mind that I got shampoo in my eyes right as somebody shouted, "Water off, water off!" and that was it. The water went off again.

I stood there for a minute shivering, before I decided to get out of the shower and get dressed. I hoped that I could rinse my hair in the sink, but when the water didn't come back on, I sprayed conditioner in my hair to dilute the shampoo.

My girlfriends could not understand why I would take a freezing cold shower.

"Why don't you just shower when you get back to your house?" they said. "Or shower at Liam's?"

"I can't," I told them. "Liam's place is twenty minutes past my house, and by the time I get there, it'll be time for dinner."

At the airport, I called Liam to let him know what time I'd be back into Oakland. He didn't answer, so I left a message.

When I got off the plane and checked my voicemail, I was disappointed that he hadn't called back. I reluctantly picked up my luggage at baggage claim, walked the long walk to the car, and drove back to Orinda. At about 7:30, I called Liam again and left another message. I tried not to sound as disappointed as I was, even attempting to sound cheerful. I never heard back that night.

The next morning, I drove to Patterson to help my parents. I was at the guesthouse when Liam called. "Hey, disregard the email I sent you," he said right off the bat. "Don't pay any attention to it."

"What email?" I asked. "I haven't looked at my inbox, so I

don't know what you're talking about."

I was so happy he'd called that I really wasn't paying any attention to his email. I figured it was in regard to what he was about to tell me on the phone.

Liam went on to explain why he hadn't called me the previous night. "This morning I was going to make a business call on my cell phone," he said. "I looked all over for it, but I couldn't find it anywhere. I just now found it in my car and heard your messages. Just delete my email."

"What email?" I said. "I haven't even opened up my computer today."

"How come you didn't call me on the house phone, like you have before?" he asked.

I felt tongue-tied. I had called him on both numbers before. At the time, I had only used my cell phone for business or emergencies. In fact, I had purchased a cell phone only because when I was married to Dale, we had been burglarized in the middle of the night while we were home asleep. We lived in happy valley suburbia, and had left the garage remote hidden in an electrical meter box for a contractor doing some work on the house; we had forgotten to take it out for the weekend. Before the burglar broke in, he cut the wires at the telephone pole and dug a hole in the grass to make sure the wires he cut went in the direction of our house, thereby severing all communication and electricity. We heard the alarm go off; it was deafening, followed by another loud noise. We flew out of bed and Dale hissed, "Get the gun, the gun, hurry."

Before I looked for the gun, I ran over to the telephone and picked it up, but the line was dead. That was the most terrifying thing of all: dialing 911 and hearing no one on the other end. Nothing. I ran over to the alarm pad and hit the buttons for Emergency/Fire, then tried to find the gun that Dale had at first hissed, and was now screaming, for me to hurry and get. My dad had given me a gun to keep in my car when I used to make long drives over mountain passes back and forth to college. The gun was in the top drawer of a very high dresser, buried under a whole bunch of lingerie. I started pulling everything out, throwing bras and underwear left and right, desperately trying to find it. It was at the very back of the drawer. I handed it to Dale, who ran and leaped forward, springing into the air with arms outstretched, hitting the floor on his stomach as he sailed out onto the landing outside our bedroom, rolling over a bit onto his side as he slid to a stop, still holding the gun. It was a two-story house, and from the landing outside the bedroom, you could look down onto the entry hall and the front double doors of the house. I peeked around the bedroom door and looked down. You could smell this person before you could even see him. He was a dark figure with a hooded sweatshirt and a knapsack over his shoulder. Tucked under his arm was a red flashlight. It was an eerie sight, and the smell was extremely strong. I had never smelled anything like it. Dale fired a shot, I closed my eyes, then opened them to see that fortunately, he had missed, and the guy made a run for it out the front door. The police later told us that the smell was most likely crack cocaine, and that's what makes criminals able to act superhuman and bust through doors and jump heights beyond regular human capacity. That is when the policeman told me to get a cell phone and a dog. And I did. I got a cell phone and a Doberman pinscher.

I didn't tell Liam that whole story, but I did tell him that the reason I'd called his cell phone was because that was the last number he'd called me from. In any case, it felt good to know that he had not purposefully blown me off. At the same time, I did feel a little let down after all that, only to end up with each of us waiting and hoping for the other one to call.

A couple of days later, I was back in Orinda and we made a lunch date for Saturday. I couldn't wait for Liam to come pick me up. I wore navy shorts with a sleeveless white top, and a white bra with pretty lace straps, just in case they peeped out of my shirt.

By this time, I had noticed that Liam paid a lot of attention to women, and specifically to their clothing and body type. He was an aesthete in every sense of the word. He had recently commented on my bone structure, and in particular, on my neck and collarbones. He told me that in college he had studied to be a sports physical therapist, before a buddy talked him into switching majors to accounting for the higher income potential. When Liam told me that I had a naturally beautiful bone structure, and said it with such confidence, it made me feel appreciated in an extraordinary way. His compliments heightened my awareness of my own femininity. This heightened awareness was a strange and new phenomenon, which added to Liam's allure.

At 11:30, Liam rang the doorbell. I dabbed a touch of Kai perfume oil behind my ears and ran down the stairs. When I opened the door, Liam gave me a hug and a quick kiss, as always. "You smell so good," he said as he brushed his cheek against mine. He stopped when he got to my diamond studs.

"Ouch, what do you have going on there?" he said.

I pulled away, feeling self-conscious and embarrassed.

"Are you ready to go to lunch?" he asked, holding some magazines in his hands.

"Yes, but what are those magazines you've got there? Do you want to take those with us to the restaurant?"

"We'll look at them when we get back," he said.

And we did. On my bed upstairs in the master bedroom, we lounged and looked at a couple of *Colorado Life* magazines for travel ideas. I had kicked off my sandals, but Liam kept his shoes on, maintaining a sense of formality. One magazine had a map on the inside cover, and Liam talked about where we were going to go on a road trip. Lying on the bed next to him, talking about our future trip, signified more than just taking in the spectacular scenery. It also meant that we would be spending quality time together.

Liam talked at length about the mountain passes across the Continental Divide. He had worked in those areas and owned a home in Tucson. He had maturity and sophistication, but at the same time he appreciated the mountains and blue skies with puffy white clouds, and the awe-inspiring travel possibilities right here in the US, all within driving distance. He had never been out of the United States, but he sure knew the layout of the land in the Western states and the Midwest. I really liked that about him. I talked about going to Chama in Northern New Mexico, close to Colorado, where my parents had gone elk-hunting with friends when I was in high school. For many years, right after the nut harvest in October, my mom and dad's mini-vacation would be to take long drives either to Utah, to visit Bryce Canyon or Zion National Park, or to Arizona to see the Grand Canyon, or to New Mexico to stay in Chama.

The last road trip they took after harvest, about eight months earlier, my dad was driving and my mom was reading the map; she had always been the designated map reader, but this was the beginning of the advancement of her Alzheimer's, and she got them lost and they ended up in the wrong place. Finally, my dad took the map and figured the route out himself.

To top off this final trip, when they stayed at The Lodge at Chama, the owner, who remembered my dad from a previous stay, gave them a large, majestic room that he kept reserved for himself or close friends. It had a stack of firewood beside a large stone fireplace. In the middle of the night, while my dad was sleeping, he was bitten by a black widow. Half of his hand between his thumb and forefinger swelled up to twice the size of his other hand, and he became dizzy and nauseous; he said it was hard to drive. After he saw the distinctive web, he surmised that the black widow had probably been in the firewood.

My next few dates with Liam melted into one another. As I entered Liam's condo one evening, I noticed that he had lit candles on the staircase landing. Astrud Gilbert and Stan Getz's "Girl from Ipanema" was playing in the background, and as I walked into the living room, I saw four guitars set out in a semicircle; each was resting on a guitar stand, with a foot rest and music sheets. After we talked a bit and exchanged a few hugs and kisses, Liam, who was always the one to pull back and say, "We'll have time for that another day," gestured toward the sofa for me to sit down.

He picked up each one of his guitars and described what kind it was, when he'd bought it, why he'd bought it, and what he liked to play on it. He had two kinds of Martin acoustic guitars: one twelve-string and one Brazilian Rosewood. He also had a white Fender Stratocaster electric guitar that looked like it came right out of an Elvis show. The last one was a Les Paul Gibson, a fave for rockers, which was super heavy when I picked it up.

I could hardly wait for Liam to start singing, but I waited patiently and got into how each guitar had its own way about it. I liked the twelve-string and how the sound shimmered, especially on the Martin Rosewood; it had a choral effect that was pleasing to the ear. Some guitars Liam plucked with his fingers, and others he strummed with a pick. On the Martin Rosewood guitar, which became my favorite, he played a song by Greg Brown called "Canned Goods," which was about canning peaches in the summer. Liam's voice sounded soft and natural, and he sang calmly and lightly, like a true serenade. I loved it.

Another time at his condo, we watched a movie and had salad and pizza delivered. After the movie, Liam brought a large tub of water into the living room and told me to put my feet in to soak. He massaged my feet with peppermint oil, without expecting anything in return. He did not jump all over me and jostle me around like a football player. Nope, he kissed me afterward, asked if I enjoyed the massage, and said that it was getting late. Hannah would probably be calling me, he added, and I ought to get home. Hannah and Cody both called me every night, and I was glad that Liam accepted and supported my closeness with my children. He would tell me to call him when I got home, but it seemed that he always called me while I was still driving. Then he would make sure that I got safely into my house and say, "Sweet dreams, talk to you in the morning."

Those summer days with Liam gave me so much energy. Days became brighter. I felt like I had been living in a black-and-white movie that all of a sudden, halfway through, became color. Like in the 1939 classic *The Wizard of Oz*, which was filmed in sepia tone up until the point where Dorothy arrives in the Land of Oz. After that, the movie was filmed in three-strip Technicolor. As Dorothy gazes out the window, the picture turns from brownish to fully saturated levels of rich color. Those first few frames of the film had been hand-painted to make for a smooth transition, purposefully giving it the "Over the Rainbow" effect. And over the rainbow is just where I was headed that summer and beyond. Color so bright and beautiful you could feel it. Color that was tangible.

One hot day in August, when the temperature reached 102 degrees, Liam was in Patterson to see a work account. After his meeting, he came over to my parents' guesthouse. My mom walked over to visit. Even with the progression of her Alzheimer's, which became more visible each day, she was still on fire with her congenial personality. As I watched Liam's blue eyes light up, his head bent forward in an eager manner, it was apparent how easily and naturally they conversed.

Liam changed from his suit and tie into more casual clothes for dinner. I had put on a navy blue dress with short sleeves. He had brought one set of clothes to change into: jeans and a navy shirt. In the beginning, when we went on dates, he would be dressed in either the same-colored shirt, or a complementary color to either the dress or skirt I was wearing. It appeared as if we had coordinated our clothes, and yet we hadn't. This happened three or four times.

When Liam and I got back from dinner, we lounged on the sofa in the living room of the little house, talking and holding hands between soft, sweet, purposeful kisses. Sitting next to each other, we looked out the window past white pillars to the aqua blue swimming pool, which was surrounded by white decking and sandstone planters filled with pink flowers. The flowerbeds were planted with deep pink, tree-shaped oleanders; hot pink geraniums; and cameo pink peonies interspersed with fragrant, pale yellow jasmine. The whole area was enclosed within a wall of white slump stone. With its Spanish terra-cotta roof, the house looked like a Mediterranean retreat. The windows were open to let in the warm breeze, which during summer in the valley felt tropical, similar to a Southern European sirocco wind. It was a hot night that only got hotter. The little house became a villa, and I felt as though I had been transported to the Italian Riviera, complete with Frank Sinatra singing "Summer Wind."

The sultry wind, the smell of jasmine, and the feeling of Liam's body on top of mine was spellbinding. It felt like we were having sex without actually having sex.

Liam left a little before midnight and called me on the way out the long driveway. We talked on the phone until he got home.

The next day, my dad chuckled and said, "I noticed the Irishman pulled outta here kinda late last night."

I didn't even comment. I only wondered if my dad had heard anything, because I knew the windows were open. While he seemed disapproving, my mom did not. "Liam is so good-looking and charismatic," she said, not long after meeting him. "He's a man's man."

It made me happy to know that my mom saw in Liam what I saw in him. I trusted her judgment.

After that night, things started changing. There was definitely an uptick in our conversations about living life with another person. One afternoon in particular, when Liam called, he asked what I was doing, and we shared a few things about the day. Afterward, he said, "That's one thing about being married and together, a person doesn't worry or get anxious about what they're going to be doing that evening, or the next day or week. It's nice to know that you have someone to spend time with. There's no guessing." It warmed my heart to hear him say that, because I found myself wanting to be married again, but only to someone who shared common interests and perceptions of life, and had a reverence for God. I thought I had found that in Liam.

Liam and I settled into a comfortable routine of at-home date nights. He introduced me to Larry David's hilarious HBO series, *Curb Your Enthusiasm*. At times we laughed until our sides hurt—the kind of laughter so infectious that the second you get a hold of yourself, you burst out laughing again at the thought of it. It was also during this time that we started talking about how nice it would be to wake up every day together.

One night, at my home in Orinda, after I had cooked a dinner of filet mignon and wild rice, Liam told me that his parents had gotten divorced two years after they were married.

"How old were you?" I asked.

"Six," he said. "I could never understand why they waited until I was four years old to get married, only to get divorced two years later."

"We have something unusual in common," I said.

"What's that?"

"My parents also got married when I was four years old."

"Well, that is some coincidence," he said.

"It sure is."

We sat there in silence as the revelation sank in, and we both felt a new sense of closeness. Later that night, with Van Morrison's "Tupelo Honey" playing in the background, we kissed on every Oriental carpet in my home. I had five or six that I thought added warmth and elegance. Most of them were Persian, the soft pile woven kind in jewel tones; a couple of them had floral motifs and a medallion in the center, and some had geometric patterns that repeated over the entire surface of the rug.

In between kisses, lying together on a navy and burgundy carpet with a royal crest, Liam said, "Wouldn't it be nice to do this every night. We could if we were married."

"I would love that," I said.

After that night, all of those carpets became magical. Liam and I referred to it as "The Night of the Magic Carpet Rides."

I thought I'd found my soulmate.

6

Haze

A month later, Liam's son Regan came to visit from Utah.
Liam had told me that he hadn't seen much of his children
since they were very young, when he and their mother had
divorced. He said he'd tried to visit them when they were little,
but that when he would go to pick them up, they would be
gone. "How can a two-year-old ride off on his bicycle?" Liam
looked at me and said. His ex-wife had even changed their last
names to their stepfather's. It broke his heart, Liam said, to see
his kids suffer.

"It's just like the story of Solomon and the two mothers,"
he said.

"What do you mean?" I asked.

"In the Old Testament," he said, "when two women both
declared that the same baby was theirs, King Solomon, the
judge, ordered the baby to be cut in half. When he told
someone to go get his sword, one of the women cried out
and said, 'Please spare the baby, and let my rival care for it.'

Solomon knew then that she was the real mother. I was the real parent, you see. I was willing to make the sacrifice and lose my children in order to spare them any pain."

So when Liam's youngest, Regan, who was just a baby during the divorce, came to visit before going on his mission, it was a big deal. Liam brought Regan over to my house in Orinda when they were on their way to go hiking. Meeting Regan made me feel special. Liam had not seen his son for many years, and yet he went out of his way to introduce him to me.

A few weeks later, Liam sent me an email stating that his mother's husband had died, and that he would be flying back to Illinois for the funeral. He also said that he was moving back to Tucson. This came as quite a shock. *Why would he do that?* I wondered.

I hopped in my classic jeep, a CJ5 with a stick shift that I usually kept on the farm, and drove to Alamo with a sympathy card and some of my chocolate-covered almonds for Liam to take back to Illinois. Since it was a warm day in September, I put the nuts in a mini ice chest so they wouldn't melt. He didn't answer when I rang the doorbell, so I left the nuts and the card in the mini ice chest on his porch.

The next day, Liam called to thank me for the almonds, and to let me know that he would share them with his sister and family back home. He also reiterated that when he returned, he was going to be back and forth between Tucson and Alamo, and would keep in touch. I wondered whether he wanted to slow things down, or take a break. I wasn't quite sure.

But my fears proved to be unfounded. By the time December came, we were back to dating again: emails, phone calls, dinners. He even installed a new sink in my kitchen and put together a bunk bed for Hannah's bedroom.

For Christmas I gave Liam a sweater and a framed picture I had taken of one of my family's almond orchards. I called this particular orchard, which had one plot of trees on each side of a dirt road, the enchanted forest. The almond trees were thirty-seven years old, very established, and big and tall. The sunlight filtering through the leaves gave the photo a shimmery effect. The sun shone its rays straight down to the earth from the tops of the trees, where there were openings between the leaves.

After the holidays, Liam invited me to join him on a company trip to Jamaica. Sitting on the airplane, just before takeoff, he leaned over and said, "When I move back to Tucson, will you make the drive with me?"

"I'd love to," I said.

When we checked into the hotel, we were given a room on the second floor. Liam asked if we could be moved to a higher level, as it was only six weeks after a devastating Indian Ocean tsunami, and Liam wanted to make sure we were safe. The desk attendant said no problem and gave us a room on the fourth floor. It wasn't that big a deal, but Liam's request made me feel that he was looking out for us.

A few days later, after we'd gone horseback riding and jumped on the water trampoline at Jimmy Buffett's Margaritaville, we were lying on the beach, looking out at the water from chaise lounges. Liam turned to me and said, "You know, I'm really sick of this company shortchanging me. I've been keeping track, and they're dinging every single one of my paychecks."

"That's awful," I said. "Have you talked to their accounting department?"

"Yeah," he said. "But she can't figure out what I'm talking about."

"That's too bad," I said.

Liam reached over and took my hand. "I don't mind if you want to jump on top of me," he said.

"You know," I said, blushing, "the CEO is just a few chaise lounges down."

Liam didn't seem to care. He stood up and waded into the water.

The next evening, a large group of us had dinner at the White Witch restaurant at the Ritz Carlton hotel in Montego Bay. After dinner, we crowded into a cab with another couple. Right as I slid over into the back seat, Liam whispered in my ear, "I was going to tell you I love you, but you kept talking."

My eyes began to sting, and I had to fight back tears.

Going to? I thought to myself. What did that mean? Was Liam punishing me because he thought I was talking too much?

I heard the first lines of the Faith Hill song "Just to Hear You Say That You Love Me" in my head. *If I could win your heart, if you'd let me in your heart, I'd be so happy, baby…just to hear you say that you love me.*

I didn't say another word for the rest of the cab ride.

The next morning, while we were in the hotel restaurant waiting for a table, Liam pulled me onto his lap and gave me a gentle squeeze. "You look beautiful today," he said, as he nuzzled my neck. By this time, I was numb to his withholding love one night and giving it freely the next day.

After breakfast, we went back to the room to grab our swimsuits. Looking around the room, I noticed how organized Liam kept his things. I appreciated how uncluttered and clean he was. At the end of his showers, his daily ritual was to use a light lavender and vanilla oil. He never smelled like a can of shaving cream. His skin was soft and clear and, from his days as a state champion wrestler, he had plenty of muscle underneath it. No hairy arms or hands. He told me that in the past, he had waxed his chest and various other parts. I had never heard of a man doing that before, and at the time I thought his grooming meant that he took extra special care of himself.

A couple of days later, we left Jamaica. Despite long hours on planes and in airports, we never got irritated with one another. We traveled easily and alike.

A week after we got back to California, Liam moved to Tucson. He told me there was overlap between his new job and his previous one. For the sake of his own job security, he told me, he had to take the new position with a competitor, even though he was still employed by his old company. I didn't feel that was ethical, yet I told myself that a lot of people would do the same thing.

Liam hired movers to transport his big items—dining room table, bed, desk, etc.—and after we had cleaned and vacuumed the condo, we loaded his two twenty-pound cats into the car. With their snow-white fur and cobalt blue eyes, they resembled Siegfried and Roy's Bengal show tigers. I had never met a man with such refined taste in cats.

We drove twelve hours to Tucson, listening to comedy on XM Radio, laughing until we had tears running down our faces, and talking about our future together. At night, as we drove down long stretches of highway, tumbleweeds would blow across the road and get caught in the grill of our car. Liam would calmly pull over and dislodge the weeds, only to run into a sandstorm a few miles down the road. What a difference from Dale, I thought, who drove like a NASCAR driver and told me that speed limit and caution signs were just posted suggestions. No matter what obstacles arose, Liam always knew exactly what to do, which made me feel safe and protected in his presence.

We arrived in Tucson ahead of the moving truck, and when we walked into the house, it was a complete mess. Liam had been renting his house to a University of Arizona student. The walls and doors were beat up and filthy, and red plastic party cups were strewn everywhere. The fridge looked like it hadn't been cleaned—ever. In the garage, a once elegant red velvet couch, now faded and worn, sat with junk piled up all around it. I cleaned while Liam went to work on house repairs.

Still, even beneath the layers of grime—the result of five to seven years of neglect—one could not mistake how beautiful the house was. It had flagstone floors, herringbone mahogany doors, a new master bedroom addition with high-gloss pine floors, including the stairs leading up to it, and downstairs, a remodeled bathroom with fancy showerheads that resembled a fountain. The bathroom floor and sitting area were done in tumbled Travertine tile, and the sink was a free-standing bowl with the faucet coming out of a mirrored wall; it felt like a spa at a resort. Liam had even put thought into the ambience and quality of the light fixtures. Everything was top-of-the-line.

The second house on the property, which Liam called "the studio," was a one-room guest cottage across from the water garden that he said he had plans to fix up, then rent out to a college professor as a caretaker while he was gone.

I was so excited about going to Tucson to help Liam, but I sure didn't expect to be working the entire time. Day and night, we renovated. We made one trip after another to Home Depot, fabric stores, and specialty imported tile companies. Even though I was exhausted by the time night fell, my heart and body longed for intimacy. But Liam was completely focused on repairing the house.

He told me to pick a paint color for the interior, although

he already had some swatches of lavender picked out for the bedroom, and he wanted me to choose one. I thought an entirely different color—anything but lavender—would be better, but Liam kept saying, "What about the lavender? Which shade of lavender do you like?"

And then there was a blue for the downstairs. We went through the same thing. I wasn't really choosing the color, just which *variation* of the color, but I didn't care. It was so nice to be together. Rather than being upset about our lack of physical intimacy, I was touched by the fact that he solicited my ideas and tastes.

"We're building a foundation," Liam would always say. "Like a house needs to be built on a sturdy foundation for it to be long-lasting, so too does our relationship."

My next trip to Tucson was in April for Liam's birthday. We re-covered his dining room chairs and had dinner at a popular Mediterranean restaurant. I brought him a new stash of his lavender "love potion," as I called it, and a handwritten card. He said that it was the best birthday he had ever had.

In June, he sent me an email ending our long-distance relationship. "You are there, I am here, and it's too far," he wrote. "Why don't we just go our separate ways? You date others, and I will too."

I sat there and stared at my computer, heartbroken. I couldn't bear the thought of being without Liam. First, I wrote him a two-page email outlining all the reasons we had talked about for being together, then I shortened it to one page, then half a page, then to one sentence. "If that is what you want," I wrote, "it's not what I want, but if that is what you want, then that is what it will have to be."

Three days after I sent that email, Liam called.

"Hey, what are you up to?" he asked, as if the last two emails had never been exchanged. I was happy he'd called. I felt like maybe he was testing me, and my love for him, so I didn't bring up the email.

"I don't suppose you could get a Mac so we could iChat?" Liam said, before I could even answer his first question.

I had always had a PC and never owned an Apple, but for the sake of our relationship, I went out and bought one. It took me a few weeks to get it up and running, with the iChat and the iSight camera, but once I did, I called Liam.

"Hey," I said. "I got the Apple computer."

"You did?" he said, sounding surprised. He seemed to like that. "You really purchased a Mac with the iChat?"

"Yes, I did…"

I felt my voice trail off a bit. It surprised me that he seemed so surprised.

Soon after, we started iChatting on a regular basis. He asked if I would fly out that winter for the Tucson Festival of Lights. It gave me something to look forward to, which I very much needed, because during that time my mom's Alzheimer's was rapidly progressing. I interviewed caregivers, and through an agency I found a woman named Paola. The first day she came in June was during a brutal heat wave. In fact, it was so hot that her dog actually died that day from heatstroke. By nighttime, I was exhausted from running around and showing Paola how things worked on our property. First, I'd had to explain how to do my parents' laundry, because my dad was very particular; his jeans as well as his shirts had to be folded in a certain way and put away in a certain way. After that, I'd taken Paola to the grocery store with a master list of things that I'd buy for my parents every week. My dad was also very particular about how he liked his food cooked, and how often the same dishes were made.

I explained all this to Paola, along with a list of "if this, then that" scenarios. My mom's Alzheimer's medications were increasing, and she'd started throwing up every time she ate a salad. And she loved salad. I would stay up with her sitting on the bed, holding a bowl for her to throw up in. With her Alzheimer's progressing, some things were no longer possible for her to do on her own. There was no more salad once we figured out that was the culprit, and that age and her disease were also contributing factors.

I had just gotten into bed when Liam called. I was glad to hear from him, but I must have sounded tired, because the next day he sent me an email saying he felt that I'd given him the cold shoulder the night before on the phone. I called him as soon as I read his email. He didn't answer, so I left a message explaining how tired I'd been from training the new caregiver in 105-degree heat. I also made sure to mention that I would never intentionally give him the cold shoulder.

Later, I thought, *He really is so sensitive.* I didn't mind, though, because I too was sensitive.

A few weeks later, on my birthday, Liam sent one of his endearing e-cards. He wrote a line from a Steve Miller song: "I really love your peaches..." The last thing he wrote was, "If I could wave a magic wand, you and I and Cody and Hannah would be living together in Patterson, helping your parents with the farm, away from your controlling ex."

This sped up the wheels that had already been turning in my head about moving back to Patterson. I missed my mom, and I felt a strong pull to be near her, as she was slowly losing her memories and her grip on reality. I loved driving the fields with my dad, and writing in my Almond Timeline about the days, weeks, and seasons. I felt the land was my birthright, and along with it came the responsibility to carry it on to the next generation. If my kids didn't feel that way, there would be nothing I could do about it, but at least I was doing what I thought was right. Dale kept telling me to rent out the land. My parents didn't need me, he insisted, my mom's Alzheimer's wasn't that serious, and I could hire accountants to do the bookkeeping and payroll. He said that by leaving Orinda and moving back to Patterson, I would be choosing my parents and heritage over my children.

Dale's accusations made me feel guilty, and I questioned the validity of my intentions. It wasn't an easy decision to make, but between my mom's deteriorating health and Liam's magic wand, I was willing to give up the life I knew and loved.

During that time, I served as the designated driver for my parents' annual post-harvest road trip. The plan was to end up in Chama, New Mexico, where we would meet Liam. I drove my mom and dad and Paola in my dad's Ford F-150 double cab. We first stopped at Zion National Park in Utah, then continued on to Bryce Canyon; the Grand Canyon; Page, Arizona; and on to Lake Powell.

On the third day of the trip, I was about to get into the driver's seat as usual, but my dad suddenly had the keys. *He* was driving, he said, and we were going home. *Going home?* We still had two more days planned for the trip. My heart sank as my dad pulled out of the parking lot and started driving in the opposite direction of Chama.

I felt sick. I had planned it out with Liam, and had been looking forward to us all having dinner together and going sightseeing. I sat in the back of the pickup truck, dumb-founded. I looked over at Paola. She looked back at me and mouthed, "Liam." *Oh, brother*, I thought. "What?" I mouthed back. She started to look in her purse for something to write on. I found a piece of paper in mine and handed it to her with a pencil. She wrote that when my dad had heard that Liam was going to be in Chama, he said that he wasn't, and we were going home. Paola, my mom, and my dad all had known the entire day before, all the way up to duping me out of the keys to the pickup, so my dad could make sure we went west toward California instead of east toward New Mexico.

I was so mad. I was the last to know.

7

Fickle

When I got back to California, I went to work on selling my house in Orinda. It was a pretty, two-story traditional home on a street that had originally been owned in its entirety by my former husband's family. His grandfather had named the street Stewart Dale. I'd noticed that in that area, many street names ended with "Dale." My mom had once pointed out that this was because in England, a long time ago, they named the streets according to the terrain; a dale is a broad valley in a hilly area, and that is just where my house sat. It was situated on a cul-de-sac in the suburbs right next door to Dale's aunt and uncle, half a mile from his parents' house, and only a quarter of a mile from his grandfather's house. This could feel cozy at times, and at other times it felt claustrophobic, as if there were no boundaries.

LeeAnn helped me organize the house for selling. At the same time, I started to look for a new house in Patterson. I looked at one just for fun, and then my dad found something in the newspaper. It was near the farm and had recently been remodeled. The kitchen had a Viking stove with six burners, a griddle, and a huge shelf with heat lamps for warming plates. I pretty much bought the house for the stove. As a bonus, it was seven minutes from my parents' house, which I was grateful for as my mom's condition worsened.

That fall, my offer on the house in Patterson was accepted. I still owned my home in Orinda, and when I was back there with my kids, after I'd drop them off at school, I'd go on a six-mile hike with five other women. One of them, my friend Sophia who had helped me with the online dating service, was from Ecuador. She had big, beautiful brown eyes, and when she talked fast, her accent became more pronounced. When we went hiking, every time I brought up the subject of Liam, she would get irritated.

"Why are you going to go see him again?" she once asked me, exasperated.

"Well, uh, um. Why?" I stammered. "What do you mean? I like him for all the reasons I've been telling you about for the past year and a half. And why? Why not. I don't understand why you're asking me this."

There was a long silence. Sophia slowly shook her head at me.

I stood there, wondering why she was shaking her head; it made me feel embarrassed and ashamed, and at the time, I did not know why.

"If you love someone," I said. "And they love you and want to be with you, why wouldn't you go see them? I have the means, and he doesn't right now. He lost a lot of money in each of his divorces, and having been through one myself, I can understand that. Why would I not go?"

"Because it's like you're chasing after him."

"But he's asking me to come visit him," I said. "He's making plans for what we're going to do when I'm there. How is that chasing?"

Sophia, still shaking her head, said quickly, "I don't care. He should be coming out to see you, or paying for you to fly there."

"Well, I just told you why it can't be that way."

Sophia went on to tell me about a couple of men she'd dated before getting married. They'd always flown her to wherever they were, and she expected no less. If they didn't put her on a pedestal, she wasn't going to waste her time. Part of me wanted that for myself, but I just didn't think that way. Growing up, my parents were a team. They did things for one another and made compromises. Sometimes one carried the team for a while, then circumstances changed, and it was the reverse. My mom worked in a law office as I was growing up, and even though my dad worked all the time and could be short with her, there was a love between them that at its root was unselfish. There is nothing that either one of them would not have done for the other.

A month later, Liam suggested that we take our dream road trip to the southwest. I flew to Tucson, and we drove to New Mexico on the I-10, then took highway 25 north to Santa Fe, and on to the historic winding route to Taos. We drove through remote mountain towns that had been established in the 1600s and 1700s, before New Mexico was even a territory. It was like being transported back in time. From Taos, we drove highway 285 into Colorado to Alamosa, then hopped onto 160, heading northwest to highway 50, and on into Gunnison. From there, we continued on to Montrose, then drove south on 550, and west a bit, over to Telluride. In the old mining town, we parked and took a walk. Telluride is nestled in a box canyon surrounded by spectacular mountains with snow on the high peaks. The charming Victorian-era storefronts remain from the gold and silver mining days, but inside they are modernized and have an upscale yet casual feel. We browsed several of the shops, and in an art gallery that sold paintings, sculpture, and jewelry by local artists, we looked at a Santa Fe blue glass bowl that Liam and I both agreed would look perfect as a centerpiece on his dining room table. I asked the salesperson for a card, wrote the name and price of the bowl on the back, and put it in my purse to order by phone as a future surprise.

We ate lunch at the Butcher and the Baker Cafe, then left Telluride and looped back up and stayed a night in Ridgway. The next day, driving south on 550, the views became indescribably beautiful. The scenery through Ouray and Silverton could rival any in the world. We stopped and had our picture taken next to the Ouray welcome sign that said "Switzerland of America." Having been to Switzerland on my honeymoon with Dale, which I didn't mention out loud so as not to make comparisons, I had just been thinking that we could have been in the Bernese Alps. The stretch on 550, called the Million Dollar Highway, along the Continental Divide south of Ouray, through the Uncompahgre Gorge to the summit of Red Mountain Pass, left me speechless. It was one of the most gorgeous places I have ever seen. We continued south on 550, passing through the San Juan Mountains and the majestic gold aspens, with walls of yellow, red, and green trees, down into Durango. From Durango, we headed east to Pagosa Springs, then dropped down into New Mexico, and on to Chama. After my dad had scrapped our plans to meet up with Liam in Chama, I was glad to finally be there with him.

It was always hard when Liam dropped me off at the airport, but this time I felt especially conflicted. It was hard to leave him, but it was equally hard to leave my responsibilities at home. I didn't know how much longer I could stay in a long-distance relationship.

While I was sitting at the airport, thinking about the stack of bills that awaited me at the farm, Liam called. Without thinking too much of it, I said off the top of my head, "I don't know how much longer I can do this. I miss you when we're not together." Liam didn't say a word, and quickly got off the phone.

Once I got home, his calls became fewer and farther between. He had misconstrued my offhand comment to mean that I no longer wanted to see him, which was not the case. About ten days before Christmas, I had the glass bowl that we had seen in Telluride sent to him. I tracked the package. I found out that it had gotten lost, but eventually it arrived on Friday. I was surprised that Liam had not called me when he received it, and I tried calling him that Friday afternoon and evening, but his phone went straight to voicemail. I tried again on Saturday morning, and he finally answered. During our video chat, I could see that the bowl was centered on the dining room table behind him. As he was telling me that he'd gotten the package and opened it, his cell phone rang. He looked down at the phone, and I noticed that he had a kind of smug, conceited look on his face. The phone kept ringing.

"Aren't you going to answer it?" I said.

"Oh, uh, it's Barry. I'll call him back."

Barry was Liam's best friend.

A few minutes later the phone rang again, and this time Liam answered, saying it was Barry again. I had a feeling that the first call was not actually from Barry, but the second call was. I started to get annoyed and feel a bit foolish for sending the gift, yet at the same time, it made me happy to have given him something so beautiful. He took out the card I sent with it and read the words aloud, as if it meant a lot to him, and as if I didn't know what it said. I had written the card, after all.

The next week I drove to Berkeley to see Dr. Paxton, a male psychiatrist I had been seeing for the past year. For the four years prior, I had been seeing a female psychologist from England, and through my first divorce and my mom's slow death from Alzheimer's, she had been like a mentor to me. She thought it would be good to change it up and get a man's perspective on my precarious relationship with Liam, and so she suggested Dr. Paxton. She had known him professionally for twenty years, and held him in high regard.

An intelligent, silver-haired man in tailored clothes, Dr. Paxton was not keen on Liam from the get-go. In our sessions, he would challenge me about Liam's yo-yoing and noncommittal behavior. For every question Dr. Paxton asked me about Liam's behavior, I had a good answer. Or so I thought. During this particular session, Dr. Paxton suggested that I tell Liam we should take a break. "Don't call him, but when he calls you," Dr. Paxton said, "tell him that you have been thinking it might be better to take a break from the relationship for a while."

One afternoon, not long after, Liam called about coming to visit me at Christmas. He said he was going to drive to St. George, Utah, to see his buddy Barry, and he was thinking about driving to California to see me after that. "I'm not sure, though," he said.

"I think we should take a break from our relationship," I said.

It was not what I felt in my heart. In reality, I wanted to see Liam so much it hurt. As in, *physically* hurt. He hung up on me, and that was that. Not a word. He just hung up the phone. I tried calling him right back. He used a flip phone, and I could hear him open up the phone as it stopped ringing, and then slam, bam. He hung it right back up. At the same time, I could hear Barry in the background saying, "Is that her?"

I called Liam again. The phone went straight to voicemail.

Distraught, I called Dr. Paxton. I was crying so hard I could barely talk or breathe. It took me a while to get out what I had done, and what had happened with Liam. Dr. Paxton told me to hang on, to just ride it out. "Give it time," he said. Give it time, he kept repeating. *Time?* By that point I had been giving the whole relationship so much time that I was going out of my head.

On Christmas, I sent Liam a text saying, "Merry Christmas, thinking of you."

He called me the next day around noon. I answered on the first ring. Just hearing his voice made my heart pound.

"I'm driving back to Tucson," he said. "I thought about driving to California to see you, but now I've decided to go back home."

Going against Dr. Paxton's advice, I eagerly said, "Why don't you drive here? Do you need to get back to Tucson for something?"

"No, just want to drive back."

I was devastated.

The holidays came and went. I decided that maybe I would be better off moving back to Orinda; I hadn't sold my house there. I had been in Patterson for two months, and I missed my children, my friends, and my hikes. I could just keep commuting every day to Patterson like I had before I moved.

I called the same movers that had moved me from Orinda to Patterson, and the date was set. I would have moved right away, but they didn't have any availability until the first weekend in April.

A couple of weeks after my decision to move back to Orinda, Liam called. I was elated. I got a rush of adrenaline just hearing his voice. He told me about all the things he was doing to improve and fix up the house and studio so that he could rent it out. I told him I was moving back to Orinda. He didn't say anything.

Within a week, Liam called to say he was planning to drive out to see me. He came the first weekend in February. I was thrilled, but as always with Liam, things felt precarious, as if our relationship were hanging on by a thread. I knew that he had been dating other women, and sometimes I would straight up talk to him about it. Right before he left Tucson for Orinda, he threatened not to come if I was going to talk about him dating other women. He said that he missed me, and he just wanted to hang out and relax.

"Sounds great," I said. "I can't wait to see you."

One evening in the kitchen, not long after he'd arrived, Liam walked up behind me as I was standing at the kitchen sink. He took his hands and simultaneously ran them up the sides of my body, then wrapped his arms around my waist and nestled his head into my neck. The motion of his hands running up my body gave me such a rush that it took my breath away. I turned around to face him, and we hugged tightly.

"I want to be with you," I said. "It's hard knowing that you're dating other women."

"That's it, I'm leaving," he said, and let go of his hug. "I told you not to mention that."

"Liam, please don't leave, don't go," I begged. "I'm sorry. I won't mention it again. I'm so glad you're here."

After that, things went okay. Liam left a few days later for Tucson, and made plans to fly back to see me in March, so we could celebrate his fiftieth birthday together. He made reservations at a bed-and-breakfast in Napa Valley. When the time came, I bought a vintage bottle of fifty-year-old Cabernet in honor of his fiftieth and picked him up at the airport. We had a couple's massage and a nice dinner at the Meadowood.

The next morning, lolling around in our hotel room, Liam looked at me and said, "When are we going to tell your parents that we're getting married?"

"We're getting married?" I said.

"Isn't that what we talked about before?"

"Well, yes, I would love to."

I was elated that Liam seemed to want to pick up where things had left off. It was just like the days when I'd lived in Orinda.

Not long after that, I called the movers and canceled my move back to Orinda. Liam and I set the wedding date for July, and started looking for rings together online. He told me to look at the Furrer Jacot diamond wedding bands, which were made in Switzerland. Liam had exquisite taste. They were the most beautiful rings I had ever seen.

Sadly, my girlfriends were not as happy as I would have expected them to be when they heard the news. I could sense their reservations. I knew Liam had been married three times. As I explained to them, just as he had explained to me numerous times, his ex-wives were all crazy. I truly believed that. When we'd first started dating, Liam had brought some photos to my house in Orinda and shown me a picture of each of them. They were all strikingly beautiful. All three had dark hair; two had emerald green eyes, and one had sapphire blue. Liam told me that his third wife (I would be his fourth, but my ex was going on his third, so it didn't seem that far out) had done a lot of drugs when she was younger. He said that he didn't find out until they were already married, and that the drugs had affected her brain. "She worked in the back of a men's tailoring shop, doing alterations," he said. "Barry and I met her when he took some suits in to be altered." *How nice,* I thought. He fell in love with a seemingly unpretentious, regular person with a regular job, like me. He liked her for who she was, not for her status, wealth, or sex appeal. Or so it seemed.

Liam described in detail how she would sometimes fly off the handle for no reason. She would scream at him, he told me, and he prayed that she would leave. One day his prayers were answered. When he got home from work, he walked in the front door and there was nothing left in the house except his guitars leaning against a wall. She had taken everything: the sofas, chairs, tables, dresser, bed, you name it, but left his guitars.

"Oh my gosh, what did you do?" I asked.

"I got down on my knees and said, 'Thank you, Jesus.' "

Liam told me his second wife was ten years younger than him. She really wanted children, he said, so he'd had his vasectomy reversed. She was a singer and would perform in nightclubs. He said that she would be gone for long periods of time, visiting her family and traveling in Europe. Liam said that he himself traveled a lot for work back then. He told me that he came home early one time and saw her giving the plumber a hug: a *long* hug. When he confronted her, she told him she was having an affair and that she wanted a divorce. "I was devasted," Liam said.

The stories only got worse. His first wife, he said, the mother of his four children, had been sexually assaulted as a child. This caused her to become enraged whenever she and Liam made love, until it got so bad that she could no longer do it anymore. And when she found out that she was pregnant with their fourth child, she screamed at Liam and told him to get a vasectomy. Another time, she came up to him and hit him with a hair dryer. He filed for divorce, just as he'd done with all three, he said.

Some people couldn't understand why Liam had moved to another state. What they did not know or see, which I saw, was the fact that he'd moved back to Tucson because he was dissatisfied with his previous job. It was also so he could finish remodeling his studio, so he could rent it out and move back to California, and we could get married.

We had been dating for two years already, and now we were back to what we'd been talking about all along.

8

Blue Hour

Two months before the wedding, it just so happened that my dad was selling his other Ford pickup truck. Every five years or so, he would buy a new pickup he used for rough work on the farm, and either trade in the old one or sell it outright. When I mentioned this to Liam, right away he said he would like to buy the truck. With the truck, said Liam, he could be ready at any time to go out to the field to help my dad, or go up to the cattle ranch my parents owned, parts of which were accessible only with four-wheel drive. Liam had a company car that he wanted to leave in Tucson for his business trips in the southwest. He would drive the pickup back and forth from California.

My dad gave me a price. Liam gave me a price. I suggested one in between, and they both agreed. My dad never talked to Liam about it, and Liam never talked to my dad about it. When it came time to do the actual transfer and complete all the paperwork at the DMV, Liam said, "Hey, if you could get this, I'll pay you for the truck just as soon as that check comes in from the pending settlement. You remember that CEO you met in Jamaica? I had to file a lawsuit against him. My attorney is working on it right now."

My heart sank and I felt kind of funny. "Okay," I said in as chipper a tone as I could muster.

It bothered me, and yet at the same time it didn't. I really believed he was going to pay me back, and anyway, it was a four-wheel drive pickup truck that was going to be used on the farm, something I could have bought from my dad for myself to use. Later that week, I wrote out a check from my bank account and deposited it into my dad's bank account. I got the registration, pulled the pink slip out of my parents' safe, and took it with us to the DMV, where Liam and I put the truck in both our names. We were one step closer to realizing our dream of going farming.

Liam was close to his older sister, Linda. Every Fourth of July, for several years, he went out to see Linda and her husband in Illinois. This year, for the first time, I went with him. He had talked so much about Linda and her family, and I couldn't wait to meet them. I flew to Tucson, and the next morning, before we left for Illinois, Liam said, "We're going to stop at a jeweler's here on our way out of town."

"Really?" I said.

"Yes, let's see if he has those rings we were looking at. Or something like them. And if he doesn't, maybe he can make them, since the rings we were looking at online wouldn't get here for a few months from Switzerland."

The jewelry store didn't have the specific rings we had been looking at online. I ended up describing what we wanted and drew a picture. Liam asked the jeweler if he could make them, and the jeweler said, "Yes, no problem. I do that all the time."

The saleslady brought out three different sizes of diamonds to put into the setting: a two-carat, a one-carat, and a half-carat. I chose the one-carat. It was hard to imagine the depth of the square diamond in the setting, and I didn't want the ring to look ostentatious. I'd had a gold setting with Dale, and I wanted this one to be different. When I married Dale, for some reason I wanted a great big diamond. Maybe because it was the 1980s, when everything was big. There was big hair, big shoulder pads, big cars, and even "Big Stuf" Oreo cookies. But now, with Liam, I didn't care about the size of the ring.

The jeweler said it was cutting it close for the rings to be ready in time for our wedding, which was a little more than three weeks away, but he could do it. We had been at the store for an hour and a half when it came time to pay. Because full payment was required for something to be handmade, and this was expensive, Liam and the jeweler went back and forth a bit over the deposit. Together both rings cost about $12,000. It was finally agreed that we would put down a two-thirds deposit. We were standing at the counter, and Liam said in a casual manner in front of the salespeople, as plain and simple as if he were asking me to pass the potatoes at dinner, "Can you give them your credit card? I'll be getting that check from the company, and I'll pay you back and take care of the balance when I pick up the rings."

"Oh, yes, sure, okay," I said, fumbling around in my wallet, looking for my credit cards. I was caught off guard. My mind was racing, trying to figure out which card had the most room on it. I was starting to feel apprehensive, but I couldn't quite pinpoint why. After I found the right card, I gave it to the jeweler, and we left.

In the parking lot, Liam opened the car door for me as always, and when he gave me a kiss, my anxiety instantly subsided.

"Is the ring anything like your other one?" he asked.

"No, entirely different," I said, and smiled.

But I thought to myself, *Why, oh, why, did he have to ask me to cover the cost?* Even though I truly believed that he would pay me back, it took the wind out of my sails.

"Good, let's go," Liam said with a big grin and those sparkling blue eyes, "and as soon as I get that check, I'll pay you back. You're the best, baby. I love you."

We were off on our road trip to Illinois. We stopped for a night in Oklahoma City, where we ate dinner at the Iron Star Urban Barbeque. The restaurant was a mix of fine dining and comfort food, and it had those exposed brick walls I love, and wood floors like at Il Postino. I ordered the beef tenderloin well done, and Liam ordered the same. *What a relief,* I thought, *that he liked his steak well done too.* "Dale used to give me so much grief for eating my meat well done," I told Liam. "He'd say it wasn't the olden days. I'm not sure why he cared so much, but at dinner he always made a big deal of it."

"Well, that's good," Liam said. "I don't want to be anything like your ex."

The next day, we continued on to his sister's house. We drove through beautiful green fields of cornstalks topped with shiny, silvery white tassels, and passed gigantic red barns. The scenery looked like those award-winning photos in glossy agricultural magazines. We stopped for chicken nuggets and some chocolate starlight mints that we bought at an old-fashioned candy store; we were each getting tired and hungry, and eating snacks helped. As I handed Liam a chicken nugget, he looked over at me and shook his head a bit.

"It doesn't matter what my sister says," he said. "I'm going to marry you."

I didn't know what he meant, so I said nothing.

We arrived at his sister's house that night. The first thing she said was that I looked like their mom, which I took as a compliment, given the photos Liam had shown me of their late mother. When Linda and Liam went downstairs for a moment, her husband, Walt, looked at me and said, "I've been rooting for you all along."

I felt my heart beat harder. "Oh, what?" I stammered.

"You were raised on a farm. I liked all the things Liam told us about you when he first met you."

"That's nice," I said. "Thank you."

Walt's compliment made me feel a bit uncomfortable, because it was bittersweet. What was I supposed to say to that? It confirmed that I was right about my hunch: Liam had been dating other women all along.

Linda and Walt had a classic two-story lakefront house. The lush green lawn in the backyard sloped down to the water's edge. A pier jutted out over the lake, which was deep and beautiful, and lined with houses all along its shores. The next day, Liam and I took the boat out right off the dock, and he officially proposed to me out on the water. Surprisingly, it felt odd; I almost wanted to stop him because it sounded so forced. He asked me to marry him without any emotion or feeling behind the words, as if he were merely fulfilling an obligation. By that point, we had talked about marriage so much on our iChats and on the long drive to Illinois—never mind that we had just bought the rings—that when Liam proposed, it felt more like a formality than a heartfelt proposal. Nevertheless, I said yes.

On the Fourth of July, we watched Walt set off sparklers from the screened-in porch, and I was astonished by the fireflies, which added to the sense of romance and nostalgia. Having grown up on the West Coast, my only experience with fireflies was from reading the P. D. Eastman book *Sam and the Firefly* to my children.

The morning we were to leave, Walt and Liam stood talking in the kitchen, and as I came up the stairs, I could tell they didn't hear me. I stopped to listen when I realized that Walt was asking Liam how his finances were. Liam quickly replied, "Fine." Walt had a big, boisterous, friendly voice, and he said in a fatherly way, "You're okay now? You been able to build yourself back up?" I heard Liam quietly say, "Yeah, it's all good now."

I immediately thought about his last divorce, and each subsequent one. Divorces are ugly, and no one wins; everyone loses. That conclusion quieted down my brain, which kept rattling on about the wedding rings. I could certainly help with the cost, I thought. Liam must have lost everything and had to pay off Janet, his last wife, in the process. Or so I thought.

After leaving Linda's, Liam and I drove to Kansas City, Missouri. We stayed one night there, and the next day he took me to the airport, where I flew back home to California. Liam went on to see a couple of accounts on his way back to Tucson.

Now that our wedding was truly official, I had to tell my parents.

When I told my dad that Liam and I were going to get married, he acted in a way I had never seen him act before. Ever. He yelled for hours.

"What in the hell are you doing?" he said, outraged. "You think you're pretty smart, huh? That guy is a no-good, lazy asshole with a big fat butt. He's a flimflam salesman. Can't you see that? You really think he's going to help you? Why are you doing this to me and your mom? This is just what happened to Grandpa and Grandma Bennett. Two of their daughters married two guys who thought they were going to farm, and Grandpa and Grandma were constantly bailing them out and saving them from one bad decision after another.

"I have saved and saved our money," my dad continued. "And worked night and day to have what we have. Please don't marry that guy. Live together, date, you don't have to get married. Why do you want to get married? You've already been married. Look how that turned out."

It was heart-wrenching to see my dad so upset, yet at the time nothing in the world, not even wild horses, could have dragged me away from Liam. I had also made up my mind a long time ago that I would never live with a man before marriage.

At my dad's insistence, I settled on going to see his cousin George, an attorney, to talk with him about drafting a prenuptial agreement. I knew Liam would never sign one. I knew that to him, signing a prenup meant starting out the marriage without trust, and trust was a huge foundation of our relationship, he liked to say. He always encouraged conversations about being trustworthy and righteous, so that there was never anything to worry about between us. How ironic, I thought years later, but that was part of Liam's game.

My dad went in thinking we were going to draft a prenuptial, and I went in to find out what the worst-case scenario would be if we *did* get divorced, thinking it might not be as bad as my dad thought, and George wouldn't have to draw up an agreement.

George's office was in downtown Patterson on a one-way street surrounded by roundabouts. I drove, and the whole time my dad kept telling me, "Turn there, slow down, turn right here." I knew how to get to his office my way, but my dad had his way. When I went his way, a hospital was undergoing a remodel, and part of the street was blocked off. "How was I supposed to know that the street was closed?" my dad said, sounding exasperated.

When I went the way I knew, there was another detour.

By this time my dad said, "That's it, take me home now. We'll call George and tell him we couldn't make it in."

After all that, I was not going home. I was glad I was driving, because I got us there, but not without a few rants from my dad, and some verbal sparring back and forth.

As we walked into George's office, my dad still annoyed and irritated, he said, "Sorry we're late. Virginia made a couple of wrong turns out there on those one-way streets, it was a mess, and with the construction and all…"

In my own defense, I said, "I did not make a wrong turn. I turned where you told me to turn, and then other…"

My dad interrupted. "Stop arguing," he said. "We can finish arguing about it when we get home. Right now, let's get to the point here."

"Okay," I said, chuckling at my dad's dry sense of humor. As if we would really finish arguing about it when we got home.

After forty-five minutes, George concluded that because of "separate property" laws in California, our family's property would not be at risk. In my worst-case scenario, it sounded like we could handle the cost. It wouldn't be good, but I didn't see it as bad enough to outweigh the emotional damage and negativity that could come with a prenup.

When my dad and I got home, I was in the kitchen making sandwiches for him and my mom. He had gone to change his clothes to go back down to the field and get on a tractor. He walked into the kitchen and said, "I just took out my black dress shoes to polish for the wedding, and pulled out some dress pants and a shirt. I'll be ready."

I looked at him and smiled. "You did?"

He nodded and smiled back, repeating, "I'll be ready."

9

Fair

The month before the wedding, I bought my dress at an upscale boutique in Orinda. I tried on a lot of different styles, but nothing seemed right. Finally, the buyer for the store pulled out a beautiful dress with dupioni silk on the top three quarters, and wide velvet trim around the bottom. The whole dress was the color peach. Peach like the book Liam and I had read, peach like the color of the outfit I wore the day I'd brought him the peaches, which was, he later told me, the day he discovered he was smitten with me. It was perfect.

The courthouse wedding was scheduled for 11:00 a.m. on a Friday, with lunch to follow at 12. Liam and I had planned it that way, as this would be the most convenient for my dad. He would be off the tractor only for a few hours, and he'd have to eat lunch anyway. I knew summer was a busy time in the fields, with the disking, spraying, and irrigating, so I didn't want to make it any harder on my dad than it already was.

The week before the wedding, I kept busy putting the favors

together. For each guest, I put a large See's chocolate truffle in its own box, which I tied with white satin ribbon. I gathered up some antique silver candle votives that were family heirlooms, which I planned to set out on the table. I filled my grandmother's Lalique crystal candy dishes with pastel-colored peppermint white chocolate nonpareils to put out at the restaurant, and I hired a florist to deliver three rectangular clear glass centerpieces filled with white tulips. We had rented a private room with one long table that seated eighteen, so that was the number of people I invited. The restaurant was on the way to the courthouse, and as I drove to my wedding, with Hannah and Cody in the back seat beside one of my college girlfriends and her kids, I called the event coordinator to arrange the drop-off. It was literally at a stoplight in front of the restaurant that I jumped out, opened up the back of my car, and handed the wedding favors and table decorations to her right there in the middle of the street. My kids thought that was pretty funny.

Once at the courthouse, I stationed Cody at one entrance and one of Liam's friends at another to make sure my dad knew where to go. Paola, the caregiver, had driven my mom in one of my dad's trucks, but for some reason, my dad had not come with them. I kept asking Paola where my dad was, and she said he was coming. We all decided to go on in, but we kept looking out for my dad. I realized he knew the courthouse and could probably find the downstairs area where we were gathered. My dad's cousin George, and his wife, Olivia, who had been my mom's tennis partner for eighteen years, were there, along with my friend Sophia from Orinda, and her husband. As I looked around, I noticed that all of the ladies were wearing some shade of blue: royal blue, navy blue, light blue, sky blue, gray blue, periwinkle, turquoise, and Tiffany blue, which my mom was wearing.

It was now 11:15, and my dad was still not at the courthouse.

Eleanor, my mom's best friend, called me on my cell phone and said, "Where are you? I was down there in the basement of the courthouse, but no one was there, so I left."

"Oh, no, please, come back," I begged Eleanor. "We're on the first floor, one up from the basement. I'm still waiting for my dad, and I won't start without either one of you here."

"Okay, I'm on my way back," she said.

"Thank you so much, I love you."

Eleanor was like a second mother to me. She was my mom's best friend and my best friend's mom growing up.

By 11:20, when my dad still hadn't shown, I asked Paola where he was for the fifth or sixth time. "I don't know," she said dismissively. "He told us to go on ahead."

"What did you just say?"

That was it, I thought, *I have to call my dad.* What if something had happened to him? He'd told me he was coming. When he didn't answer his cell phone, I called Jim, one of the guys who worked on the farm. "Have you seen my dad?" I asked. "I'm worried, I've been calling him, and he isn't answering his phone. He's supposed to be somewhere right now."

"Yeah, I'm looking at him," Jim said with a know-it-all manner. "He's on the tractor disking the row across from me."

Well, at least he's okay, I thought.

"Can you please get his attention?" I said. "I need to talk to him."

"He's not getting off the tractor, I can tell you that. I told him what time it was and where he should be right now, and he said he isn't going."

"What?" I said in disbelief. "He told you he's not going?"

"You know how your dad is. Once he's made up his mind,

that's it," Jim said.

I could hardly accept what I was hearing. "Okay," I said, and hung up the phone.

I looked at Liam, who was standing right next to me. I fought back tears, blinking as hard as I could while looking up to stop them from rolling down my cheeks.

I marched over to Paola. "I just called Jim," I said, "and he said my dad isn't coming."

"I told you he's not coming," she said flatly.

I was so mad I almost screamed.

"You've been telling me for the last forty-five minutes that my dad was coming, and now you're telling me he's not? You've known all along that he wasn't coming, and you've been lying to me, and I've been standing here waiting and waiting, looking like a fool. Why didn't you tell me?"

The din of noise that up until that point I could hear all around us completely stopped. Everyone was looking at me. Not a sound except for me scolding Paola.

She just sat there with a deadpan look on her face. "I told you he's not coming," she repeated flippantly.

"You did not once tell me that my dad wasn't coming," I said. I was so angry, but I reined it in and continued. "Every time I asked you, 'Where is my dad?' you said he's coming and to go on ahead, he would be there. If I hadn't called Jim and found out from him that my dad wasn't coming, when were you going to tell me?"

Paola just shrugged her shoulders.

I turned around and walked off, looking for Liam. Paola stayed seated as if nothing had happened. She could have said something, anything, but instead she just kept leading me on. Of course, it was my dad's fault, but someone should have just told me the truth. Once again, I was the last to know.

I walked over to Liam, who was my rock, and said quietly and sadly, "He promised me he was coming. He told me he'd polished his shoes." Liam grabbed my hand and squeezed it. I didn't want to take away from Liam's happiness, or this special moment in our lives. I tried to smile; it was hard, but looking at Liam, I let the feeling of peace he brought wash over me.

"It's okay, it's going to be alright," Liam said. "He'll miss it later. It is what it is."

As we started to assemble in the jury services area on the first floor of the courthouse, where the commissioner was directing us to stand, and as the guests began to take their seats, Eleanor walked in. I was so happy to see her. I knew then that we could start the ceremony. The Deputy Commissioner of Civil Ceremonies officiated.

A likeable and robust man in his mid-sixties, the commissioner started by reciting wedding vows that he had written himself. "A ring is a circle," he began. "A circle is the symbol of the sun, of the Earth, of wholeness, of perfection, and of love. It is worn on the third finger because of an ancient Greek belief that a vein from that finger goes directly to the heart. No matter what we encounter, we will encounter it together, and we will emerge as one." Next he had us repeat this vow to one another: "I vow that this love will be my only true love, and I will make my home in your heart only, from this day forward."

When it came time to recite the actual vows, Liam perfectly repeated word for word after the commissioner. When it came to my turn, though, I froze. I don't know if it was because I was still shaken up, or nervous, or not paying attention, but when the commissioner looked directly at me and said, "Now, repeat after me," I didn't know how to follow his instructions. I wasn't sure if I was to repeat word for word, or to wait until the end and try to say it all together. Liam gently tapped my elbow, and people gasped a bit.

It was the sound of my kids giggling that snapped me back into the present. "I'm sorry," I said to the commissioner. "Could you read that over again?" He did, and I repeated after him, this time breaking it down into shorter sentences. After I repeated the vows, we quickly exchanged rings, kissed, and it was done. We were married.

We posed outside by the rose garden for photos, then walked straight down to the restaurant, an authentic Italian eatery. I had preselected three meals the guests could choose from, so as to shorten the lunch overall. I didn't want to hold people up.

When the bill came, I looked it over as everyone carried the tulip centerpieces up the stairs. I had made the reservations and was the contact for the lunch, so I thought, logically, *I guess it's me paying for it.* But I couldn't help but wonder: *Where was Liam?*

People disbanded, and our friends and my kids went back to the house to pack up. For some reason, Liam hadn't asked his kids to the wedding. When I asked him why, he shook his head at an angle, mouthing a silent, "No." I never did feel a need to push for a response because of what he had told me about their mom, and how she had alienated him as a parent. At the time, it just didn't seem that important. We'd planned for the adults to go over to the Claremont Hotel in Berkeley, where we were all staying overnight and going into San Francisco for dinner. My kids, along with my friend Sarah's kids, would be staying with extended family.

The Claremont Hotel, built in 1915, is an iconic luxury hotel. A California landmark with sweeping views of the San Francisco Bay, it was originally designed as a romantic castle at the start of the Gold Rush, and later became a grand hotel. That evening we all had drinks in the lobby bar overlooking the Bay, then jumped into taxis for the twenty-minute ride into the city. Liam had told me to make reservations at Plouf, a trendy French bistro on Belden Place in the Financial District. Lined with French restaurants with crowded tables abuzz with chatter streaming out onto the alley beneath miniature white lights, Belden Place has the feel of a narrow street in Paris.

When the bill came, Liam, who was sitting close beside me, looked it over. "Do you think this looks okay?" he asked. Before I could answer, his friends Greg and Susie grabbed the bill and said they were going to buy dinner.

The next day, we all had brunch together at the hotel restaurant. In addition to serving the finest food, The Meritage restaurant inside the hotel, has two-story-high ceilings with price points to match. When the bill came, Liam grabbed it and leaned over my shoulder. "We need to get this," he said quietly. "They bought us dinner last night."

"Let's just put it on the room," Liam said. So that's what we did.

Later that same morning, as Liam and I checked out at the front desk, I noticed that the dark-haired young woman who was helping us had on a wedding ring just like mine. Only hers was gigantic and looked to be at least four carats. This was an unusual setting to start with, and to have this woman assist us, out of all the people who could have checked us out, seemed like an odd coincidence. At the same time that I was observing this, I looked over at Liam; he had noticed, too. He looked over at me and tipped his head down toward her, raising his eyebrows at the same time, gesturing to her ring.

"Oh, my goodness," I said to her. "Your ring is beautiful."

"Thank you, I just got engaged. My fiancé picked it out and bought it for me," she gushed.

Hearing that made my heart sting. I felt more than ever that I couldn't tell any of my friends that I had bought my own wedding ring, so I just buried it a little deeper in my psyche.

"It's beautiful," I said, admiring her ring. I held my hand out over the counter to show her mine. "Look," I continued, "I have the same wide band with the raised matte platinum setting and princess-cut diamond. It's a smidgen of the size of yours, of course, but what a coincidence that they're so similar. Especially for such an unusual setting!"

As we walked away from the counter, Liam asked, "Why didn't you choose a larger diamond?" I found this odd, because he had always seemed so unimpressed with jewelry. In fact, one time, he'd even said, "We're not jewelry people." I wanted to reply, "We're not? Who said we're not?" But for some reason, my brain kept lingering on the *we* part of that statement, and I didn't say anything. Besides, I was the one who had ended up paying for the whole set. Both of our wedding rings had gone on my card.

In order for the rings to get to California from Tucson in time for our wedding, they'd had to be shipped overnight. Liam had driven from Tucson, which took a couple of days, and so he'd had to leave two days before the rings were to be delivered by the jeweler. Those two days made a difference in the timing. If Liam had waited for the rings to be ready, he would not have made it to the rehearsal dinner the night before our wedding.

The week before the wedding, the jeweler had called to give me an update. He said they had rushed the job and it was a push for them to get it done in time. "We'll send it out the second it's finished," the jeweler assured me. "We've got your credit card on file, and we'll put the remaining one-third balance on there. Best case will be to send the ring overnight Wednesday, to arrive on Thursday morning. In case you need to make any adjustments, you'll still have time to take it to another jeweler in California. I can call an associate I know in the area to help expedite, if necessary."

After all the jeweler had told me, it seemed unnecessary to say, "No, I'll have Liam call you back with *his* credit card." To bring up changing payment arrangements distracted from the urgency of getting the rings made. Besides, at that point, I had no reason to believe that Liam would not pay me back.

While we stood in the lobby, checking out of the Claremont, Liam's friends came up to the counter to check out also. I had my credit card in my hand, since I had made the reservations. Once again, Liam smiled and in his soft, smooth voice, he said, "I'll pay you back for all this once I get my settlement."

At the same time, touching his friend's hand in a gentle push back, he said, "Hey, we got this. Put your wallet away."

"No, no, no," his friend, Greg, said. "We'll get our room."

Liam was insistent. "Put your wallet away," he said for the second time.

Just then, another couple walked up to the counter. I couldn't believe it, but Liam said the exact same thing to them, smiling away with his pearly whites. The next person to walk up was my friend Sarah, and Liam told her the same thing, too. *Was the host couple obligated to pay for everything for everybody?* I wondered. *Maybe Liam and I could have talked about this beforehand.*

My farming family was frugal; not miserly, but frugal. They made their money working outside in hundred-degree heat, hoeing beans, and working in the orchards to bring in the crops. Once, when my mom and dad were first married, my mom was helping my dad pick up almonds after they'd been shaken off the trees during harvest.

"How much do you get paid for these?" my mom asked my dad.

"I don't know," my dad replied.

"You don't know how much you're going to get paid?"

"No, we just grow them, and take what they pay us."

That was how farming was, and still is, depending on the crop and the buyer. Sometimes we get paid only once a year, or sometimes never, because the buyer declares bankruptcy, or the crops are wiped out due to the weather, or there are dock strikes, or global economic issues. I grew up with my grandpa telling me what it was like to live during the Great Depression, and since you never knew what Mother Nature had in store, he would say, you must always keep enough money on hand to float you through a bad year or two.

I was not used to this big spender feeling I was experiencing with Liam, and I wasn't sure how I felt about it. His fervor about spending my money made me uncomfortable.

Oh well, I thought. *What was it all worth if I didn't have someone to share it with?*

For the first week after we got married, my dad called every morning at 6:00 a.m. He would ask Liam and me to go out to breakfast, and we did. Nothing was ever said about the fact that he hadn't come to the wedding. Time went on as if nothing had happened. Shortly after the wedding, Cody asked me, "Mom, how can you talk to Grandpa after he didn't go to your wedding? You're his daughter. How could he have done that?"

I told Cody that I knew he hadn't come to the wedding based on principle, not because he didn't love or support me. It was true that my dad didn't agree with the marriage, and was not going to participate in something he didn't agree with, but I forgave him because I didn't take it personally. He was operating from his principles.

In the beginning, married life was sublime. Liam was very affectionate, always giving me a hug or a kiss, if we each had been out somewhere. He was caring, patient, courteous, and tidy. Never once did he leave the toilet seat up. Lid always closed. In fact, I was the one who one time didn't put the lid back down, and I got a gentle reminder that the cats might fall in. Liam clipped his finger and toenails outside, and always hung up his clothes. Everyday life was idyllic. I felt an irresistible pull toward him, as if I were the north pole of a magnet and he were the south pole. No matter how far apart we were, a force pulled us together.

During the day, when things got harried on the farm, or daily life felt overwhelming, I would think about going to bed with Liam that night, lying beside him, his arms wrapped tightly around me, and everything would seem alright.

During intimacy, he would tell me that people didn't usually make love for three to four hours like we did. Our sexual chemistry was off the charts.

I didn't know it then, but I was under Liam's spell.

Little by little, though, my heart grew heavier with each new request for money. It had started before we'd even gotten married, and unbeknownst to me a precedent had been set. After the wedding, I did not tell my girlfriends that I had bought my own wedding ring. Part of me knew it wasn't right, and I didn't want to hear their admonitions. And since Liam had assured me that he would pay me back, I justified it to myself. So, at the beginning, my husband's recurrent and often lavish spending via my bank account was my secret.

10

Sunshowers

A few weeks after Liam and I were married, there was another big heat wave and he complained that the air conditioner wasn't good enough. "It's so hot here," he said one day, calling me at my parents' house, where I was working in the office. "I'm moving back to Tucson if we don't get an air conditioner that works better." At the time, I thought he was half-joking.

Liam proceeded to call around and had a top-of-the-line air conditioner with a whole-house fan and electrostatic air filter installed. I didn't really think to ask questions about an air conditioner. To me, an air conditioner was just that—an air conditioner. The one I had worked, but not efficiently enough, according to Liam. I didn't know that the one he had installed cost $13,000 until the installation guys were outside, waiting to be paid.

I had just taken out my checkbook, and was getting ready to write a check, when Liam said, "I made a deal with them.

If we pay them cash, they'll take two thousand dollars off, so you'll need to give them cash."

I looked at Liam. "This much money, in cash?" I said. "The bankers are going to think I'm doing drugs, or laundering money. It's a good thing I even have this much cash in my account to begin with."

This was crazy, I thought. I didn't like this situation.

"You gotta get the cash," Liam said. "They're waiting."

"Well, they can wait," I said, feeling burned. "This is a lot of money for me to just up and run to the bank and withdraw. I'll go right now, but tell them they'll have to come back later today to get it."

It turned out to be a great air conditioner, though. It kept the dust at bay, and I couldn't believe it, but there was hardly any dust for three to four days. I used to see dust in one day on the furniture. With the new system, it would take almost four days for the dust to appear again, and this was a house out in the country. But not even the air conditioner's wonders could negate the fact that, once again, I was footing the bill.

I was starting to feel like something was off, but life with Liam was so pleasurable that I ignored my inner voice. Life with Liam felt like playing house, almost like make-believe: part fiction and part reality, like we were Ozzie and Harriet on TV in the 1950s. There was no feeling of drudgery in the usually mundane tasks around the house. Everything seemed great and easy, except for the money part, which I just kept burying. I felt purposeful. Life isn't perfect and no relationship is perfect, I would tell myself. "There is always a plus and a minus to everything," my mom often said, and so that's how I saw it.

In the fall, Hannah left her dad's house in Orinda and came to live with us in Patterson. I enrolled her in an excellent public school a mile away from our house. She moved in with us, despite the fact that her father claimed it would be detrimental to her education. Because of the school's demographics, Dale said, the kids in Hannah's class would bring down her level of education, which I told him was not true at all. Yes, it was true that she would be among a socioeconomically diverse group of students. She would be in class with children of farm laborers, wine magnates, CEOs of global companies, and everyone in between. And yes, it was different from the homogeneous group of students from her previous school in the Bay Area. But this school had a long waiting list for intradistrict transfers from all over the city, and many of the teachers and special programs were highly acclaimed. Hannah's grandmother finally convinced Dale that if Hannah wanted to live with me and kept being told that she couldn't, that this would be more detrimental than anything else.

When I'd first moved back to Patterson to help my mom, Hannah and Cody had stayed in Orinda and continued at their local school. So, when Hannah moved in with us, I was ecstatic to have her back at home. Liam, Hannah, and I took trips together; we visited the Grand Canyon and the Hoover Dam. Liam designated Hannah the official photographer, helped her with her math homework, and looked up tennis academies where she could train.

I continued to buy all the household items, and was still remodeling Hannah's bedroom and bathroom when Liam moved in after we were married. When I'd bought the house, I had lived in it by myself for nine months, which is when I'd had most of the work done. I'd had a wall moved and knocked down, and updated what would be the kids' rooms. I was glad to have done this, because when the contractor knocked out the wall, he found it filled halfway from the floor to the ceiling with mouse turds. I'd installed new light fixtures, new carpeting, built-in closets, built-in desks, and gutted and remodeled a Jack-and-Jill bathroom for Hannah and Cody. Right before Liam moved in, he asked if I had a closet for him. I wondered why he couldn't share my closet, but it was easy enough to open up a hall closet into our bedroom and call it his.

We had been married for about six months when Liam's job dissatisfaction ramped up. He told me that if his company knew he wasn't living in Tucson, he could be fired. He was still able to work with his accounts, he said, but it was getting more difficult. I suggested that he look for a new job close by, or at least in Northern California. But each time I suggested this, he would adamantly shake his head and mouth the word, "No."

One night, about one in the morning, Liam got out of bed and started pacing. He went into the office, and then came back into the bedroom. I got up and sat on the edge of the bed, but when I tried to talk to him about it, it only made him angrier, which in turn upset me. I had learned from my mom how to listen and rephrase, and to let the other person know that you are trying to understand so that you can talk it out and find the best possible solution. But in this case, Liam shut me out.

Liam didn't talk about his job again until a few weeks later. One afternoon, when I came home from the farm to make lunch for us, as I did every day, I found him sitting in the office. I gave him a kiss hello, as usual. With a big smile on his face, Liam said, "I quit my job." Just like that, with no preface. Nothing. He didn't even ask how I would feel about it; in fact, he seemed giddy to share the news.

"Does your company have a territory where we live?" I asked.

"They do," he said, "but the guy who has it is established, and he's not going to give it up."

"How do you know that?" I asked. "What if he wants to retire? He might be thankful that someone who knows the company could take over right away."

Liam shook his head at that familiar angle.

Once again, I felt the wind go right out of my sails. I knew that my dad would be less likely to want Liam to work on the farm if he didn't have an outside job. They hadn't even discussed the idea, and here Liam had gone ahead and quit.

I was worried. I was already feeling pressure as the sole provider for our family, and this only added to my stress.

"If I'm going to help your dad on the farm," Liam said, "and we're going to make this go, like we've talked about, your dad is never going to ask me to help him, and I will never be able to help him, if I have another job."

I knew that wasn't the case, so I kept pedaling. "Oh, but, yes, he will," I said. "You can help on the weekends, when it's harvest, or in the evenings. My dad will see your knowledge of working on a farm, and he'll want you around more."

Liam cut me off. "It's not going to work if I have another job. This is how it has to be done. Hey, is lunch ready?" He finished with a big smile, hugged me, and said, "Let's eat."

"I need to go make it," I said quietly.

Toward the end of the year, Liam started on a few home improvement projects. First, he hired someone to hang new sheetrock in the garage, and then he called a painter, who happened to be Mormon, Liam said. After the garage was painted, Liam wanted to change the doors in the master bedroom, make the closet lights turn on when the doors opened, and remodel the outside porch. I liked how the porch looked, but Liam wanted to make the railings and columns more substantial. *How industrious,* I thought, *to improve the existing structure.* And he knew how to do that type of work. After the completion of each project, I would think, *Okay, now I'm sure he'll look for a job.* But one project led right into another, and another, and another.

Once we got into it, I was spending copious amounts of money at Lowe's and Home Depot. Liam dragged me on trip after trip to buy a skill saw; a miter saw; a circular saw; a sawhorse; power drill sanders; a drill press; a jointer; a planer; random orbital sanders; a monster fifty-five-gallon-drum shop vacuum for sawdust; chisels; wood clamps in ten different sizes; and a moisture meter for the wood. It was mind-numbing. Each time we went, he made me feel that if we didn't get a particular item, the project could not be completed and/or could not be completed to our satisfaction. Sometimes, if I asked him, "Really? Do we honestly need this?" Liam would nod his head and emphatically say, "Yes, definitely. Can't be done without it."

Then he would praise me. "You're such a wonderful wife," he would say. "There's a lot of men out there with wives who would get jealous or mad that they had a hobby, especially one that required them to work out in the cold garage till late at night to finish things." What could I say to that? It made me feel good that he was appreciative of the things I did for him, and I was appreciative of his talents. We did things for each other with unconditional love, I thought.

11

Foxy

Over the next few months, Liam and I settled into a new normal. He began to research my family tree, and even created an account with Ancestry.com. I was interested, as my family had farmed for five generations in California, and I was curious to see what he'd find. My first husband's family also had deep roots in Northern California. Dale's grandfather had bought property around the Bay Area, and Dale liked to talk about whose family's property was going to be worth more in the long run. He would aggrandize his own family's legacy, and at the same time accuse my dad of boasting.

There's an ethos to farming that I don't think Dale understood. He was a stockbroker and was used to the instant gratification of trading. Farming requires a different temperament. Due to its cyclical nature, the money often doesn't come in until after the harvest. It's like working for full a year without receiving a paycheck, then seeing the fruits of your labor materialize all at once. It takes time to grow a crop, and there is an inherent slowness to the process and to the rewards. In my family, harvesting meant more than a gathering up of the crop at one time, and more than the money that followed. Harvest represents the culmination of a year's worth of immense human effort combined with the miracle of nature to produce the crop. Delayed gratification is built into a farmer's way of life. Even though this had been an integral part of my upbringing, I did not know this concept had a name until more recently. Liam personified it. He knew the value of delayed gratification, and it drew me to him.

Liam's attention always made me feel special. At the end of the day, when I got back to the house, we would each have a glass of wine, and I would put out cheese and crackers. When I made dinner each night, he would come into the kitchen and keep me company while I cooked. He would ask me how my day went, and tell me about the improvements he was making on the house. He said he was building a new shed in the backyard to store the lawnmower, garden supplies, and Hannah's gymnastic mats. There were also two huge picture windows in the front of the house, each measuring eight by ten feet, that he said needed replacing. They were so large that to replace them cost more than $10,000.

By that time, I was becoming anesthetized to the high prices, and I wrote a check without the gut-wrenching feeling I'd had during the air conditioner transaction. I was glad that the picture windows were safer, actually, because I had always worried about them when I brought my mom over on Sundays. I was concerned that she might walk into them. Every Sunday, up until my mom began to have seizures, I cared for her from 7:00 a.m. until 5:00 p.m. I would get out of bed at 6:00 a.m., leave the house forty-five minutes later, and stop at a donut shop to buy my parents their favorite crumb cake donuts. I'd wake up my mom, put her robe and slippers on her, and bring her into the kitchen, where I made her coffee and read the paper out loud to her. Duke, her beloved Doberman, never lifted his head, or even so much as flinched whenever I walked into their house, but the second my mom came into the kitchen and sat down, that black ninety-pound ferocious watchdog turned into a full-body-wagging, hunched over, head-hanging-down puppy dog. He would gallop over to my mom, skid to a standstill, then gently put his head down onto her lap. The love that dog had for my mom, and vice versa, always amazed me.

On those Sundays, Liam never once complained. He was supportive and kind, and showed compassion toward my mom and her illness. Some Sundays, when I brought my mom over to watch *I Love Lucy* reruns or a Westminster dog show, Liam would play his guitar and sing to her. It was beautiful. My mom would tap her right foot to the beat and smile as she tried to hum along. Then, a little later, I'd sit with my mom in front of the big, eight-by-ten-foot picture window, and close to five o'clock, I'd start watching for my dad to come pick her up. I kept an extra tube of her favorite frosted coral lipstick, which I'd put on her while we sat waiting. Even with her Alzheimer's disease ravaging her brain and body, my mom always looked chic and refined. She was like a combination of Grace Kelly and Catherine Deneuve, with blue-green eyes and a trim figure. After my dad picked her up, they'd grab hamburgers at In-N-Out, and when they got back home, he'd help her put on her pajamas and brush her teeth.

At the time, I saw a lot of tenderness in Liam, and it reminded me of the tenderness that my dad had shown my mom. When Liam commented that we would do as much for each other, it solidified my hope that we saw things the same way.

In June, a month before our one-year wedding anniversary, Liam asked me for money to make the mortgage payments on his house in Tucson. I had been under the impression that his house was paid for, and was surprised to learn that he had a mortgage, since he had never mentioned one. A couple weeks later, he asked me for money for a second mortgage, which he had not mentioned when he'd asked for money for the first. Did he think that I wouldn't pay attention, or that I'd forget about the first one? Each time he asked me for a check, it would be for a different amount. When I asked him why, he would answer, "The cleaning lady was there," or, "The neighbor called, and a big tree limb went down, so I had to hire a tree trimmer to go in and clean it up." Another time, it was, "The cleaning lady said the swamp cooler went out. Had to get it repaired." I wrote each check to Liam hoping that he would soon find a job.

That same month, while he was on a short trip to Tucson, Liam called me from his dentist's office. "Can you give them your credit card?" he said.

"What?" I said.

"I just had a root canal and some work done that totaled a couple grand. I'm going to hand the phone over to DeeDee."

I gave DeeDee my card number, but after I hung up the phone, I wondered when this was going to stop. Not anytime soon, apparently, because a few days later, Liam asked for money to help renovate his son Mitch's house. Mitch and his wife had purchased a home in Arkansas close to where he would be going to law school in the fall. I would hear Liam talking with Mitch on the phone about remodeling this or that, or instructing him on how to tear out a wall and what tools to buy. Liam continuously talked in the construction terminology typical of small remodels, and thus began the multiple requests to help Mitch and his wife.

Then there was Liam's younger son, Regan. Liam had promised Regan he'd buy him new suits for his job interviews when he got back from his mission to Sweden. "Regan's young, and he needs a good start," Liam said, asking if I could help. "He spent eighteen months in Sweden, learned to speak Swedish within a month, all while living in bare-bones apartments, going door-to-door, baptizing people. That's dedication. Regan was just a baby when Annette and I divorced, and he wasn't tainted by her hatred toward me like the other kids."

So, of course, I wanted to help Regan, too.

At the end of June, we took a trip to Illinois to see Liam's sister Linda for the Fourth of July. With Regan home from his mission, and Hannah coming with us, I was looking forward to us all being together. I made the airline reservations for the four of us, but inside I felt a slight cringe. Each ticket averaged twelve hundred bucks because of connections and timing. I kept thinking that once Liam got a job, the money situation would get better.

In Illinois, we all went shopping at the Woodfield Mall in Schaumburg, and Hannah helped Regan pick out what they called "cool, casual clothes" at American Eagle and Urban Outfitters. Standing right behind me, Liam said in earshot of Regan and Hannah, "You got the credit card, right, honey? It's so generous of Hannah to give her time to Regan like this." By that time, I didn't even know why Liam bothered saying anything; it had become the norm for me to pay for every expense. No one but Liam and I knew this. I justified it with the fact that he did so much around the house, fixing things up. I figured this was his way of contributing. Plus, I'd grown up thinking it's not about who is doing more or less, it's about trying to do your best at whatever it is you're doing.

It was a fun trip, going out on the lake in front of Linda's house, jumping off the boat and swimming and watching fireworks. One morning, when I opened the door and walked out of the bedroom that Liam and I were staying in, I saw Regan kneeling by his bed, saying his morning prayers. Liam told me that this was how the young missionaries started their day. He described the Mormon prayers in the morning, evening, and in between. After seeing what an earnest and well-mannered young man Regan was, I wanted to help him that much more.

When we got back from Illinois a few days after the Fourth, Liam told me that he was going to Arkansas to help Mitch and Dana with their new home. "The house was a steal at $50,000, but it needs a lot of work," he said. "I said I'd help him fix it up."

I couldn't believe my ears.

"Liam, let *them* fix it up," I said. "*They* bought the house. *They* are young and newly married. Let *them* do that together." I kept trying to emphasize that it was their responsibility. "Plus," I continued, "didn't you just ask me to send them $3,000 to replace their front door?"

"I told Mitch I was going to help him," Liam said, ignoring my question, shaking his head with incredulity. "He's starting law school, and it's gotta get done while he still has time. This is an opportunity to build our relationship and let him know that we are there for them, just like we would help Cody or Hannah, if they needed anything."

I couldn't say much to that, because, yes, I would want to help my children, so, yes, I figured I should help Liam provide for his kids, whom he was now referring to as "ours." Since before we were married, I had told him how I'd wanted four children, and now he frequently referred to us as having six. His four, and my two.

12

Temperate

It was the seventh of July when Liam went out and bought a cover for the back of the pickup truck and started loading up tools: the circular saw, the power drill sanders, the drill press, the miter saw, and whatever else he could fit into the bed of the truck and still get the cover to close. "Wish me luck, baby," he said. "We're doing this for our granddaughter, Emily." Emily was Mitch's little girl.

At this point, our one-year anniversary was two weeks away. I thought Liam would make it back by then, no problem. A few days' driving time each way, and a week or so there, and then he'd be back. But it didn't work out that way. A week later, Liam called me sounding dismayed. He and Mitch were together in the pickup, he said, and they were trying to rent a U-Haul trailer. But because the proof of insurance in the pickup's glove box wasn't current, they couldn't get the rental. The date had expired.

"No, it hasn't expired," I told Liam. "I just forgot to put an updated card in the glove box."

As with all the other bills, I paid for the car insurance and the health insurance. When Liam quit his job, he had no health coverage, and with his hemochromatosis, I added him to my health insurance. On this same phone call, he asked if I could put another $3,000 in his bank account, because he and Mitch were replacing the kitchen cabinets, which were rotted out from the rats living in the walls. I found this a strange coincidence, given that I'd told Liam how my house once had mice in the walls, but still I thought it seemed reasonable. I went to the bank and withdrew cash from my account, then crossed the street to Liam's bank, where I deposited the cash into his account.

What had at first seemed reasonable became unreasonable when he asked me three more times to do the same thing. Five days later, Liam called to ask if I could put yet another $3,000 into his bank account. He told me that the living room and two bedrooms had asbestos hanging like flocking on a Christmas tree from the ceilings, and we couldn't have little Emily playing with that over her head. Six days later, he called to ask me for $4,500. This time it had to do with the attic and the air conditioner, and the heater and the trusses.

By now, our one-year anniversary had come and gone, and the thought occurred to me that maybe this marriage wasn't going to work. Could I really be married to Liam for only one year? I put that thought on hold and decided to fly out to Arkansas to see for myself what the heck was going on.

Liam picked me up at the airport. We drove to Mitch's house, and it was all just as he'd said, except there was so much more than we had talked about to complete. There was a two-foot drop out the living room sliding glass door that opened to the backyard. Liam and Mitch had put in stone steps and were starting to lay out some more for a small patio. Everything was about three quarters done.

"You have *got* to get another person to help you," I told Liam.

"How?" he asked.

"We get out a phone book and look in the yellow pages under 'handyman,' and start calling people, that's how," I said, exasperated. "This is crazy, Liam. You're out here in Arkansas, with at least another two to three weeks left of work. If we can hire someone to work with Mitch to finish up, that person could help him in the future with repairs, especially since he and Dana don't know anybody here yet."

The next day I flew back to California, and Liam finally found a handyman. With the Home Depot bills, the handyman, and Liam's hotel bill in Arkansas, it was still another $11,000 by the time I wrote the last check for that project. Meanwhile, I was still paying for Liam's two mortgages on his house in Tucson. When he got back to California, he suggested that "we" buy a house to flip. "I'll fix it up, and we'll make a profit. This is a great thing to do while I'm waiting for your dad to hire me." I felt a heaviness in my heart. I knew that flipping a house involved a lot of time, money, and effort, and was a lot easier said than done. But Liam persisted and convinced me that this was a sure way to make some money. Before I knew it, I was sitting in an escrow office, writing a check for a new house.

That fall, when Regan started college, I paid for his tuition and books, a refrigerator, and a car. He was the first one of Liam's kids to have their last name changed from their stepdad's back to Liam's, and I also paid for the legal fee. At the time, it made me feel good to help Liam reconnect with his children.

At the same time, Hannah started the eighth grade. After her school day ended, I would often drive her up to Sacramento for tennis academy during the week, not getting back until nine o'clock at night. On those days I made dinner in a crockpot at eight in the morning, then went to my mom and dad's to do the bookkeeping, and continued recording farm information in my Almond Timeline.

One morning, sitting in the windowless office at my dad's, I had the computer out and was concentrating on reconciling a bank statement, when I heard my mom screaming. "Stop, stop, please stop," she yelled. I jumped up and ran through the house to the bathroom. "Please don't kill me," she was still pleading loudly. "Stop." I paused for a second outside the bathroom door. I could hear the water running in the shower, and the caregivers saying quietly, "It's okay, Irene, it's okay. We're right here. Nothing is going to happen to you. We're almost done."

There are two doors to the bathroom: a main entry off the hall, and one that you enter from the bedroom. I went around to the back one and peered in. In the reflection of the mirrors, I saw my mom sitting on a chair in the shower, and one of the caregivers in the shower with her. The caregiver was barefoot with her pants rolled up. She was gently rubbing my mom's scalp with shampoo, giving her a shower. My mom was still pleading, "Are you going to kill me?" And again, the caregivers reassured her that she was safe.

The other caregiver was standing right outside the shower with a nice big white fluffy towel. I could see that my mom's clothes, which they had chosen for her, were neatly laid out, and her slippers were right there waiting. All looked good to me. I saw that the caregivers were taking special care of my mom. What they didn't know was that my mom never got her head wet when she went swimming. She hated to go underwater. My parents had a pool in the backyard, and no matter how hot it was, when she went out to the pool to cool off, she never went past the third step. For all of my life, I'd known that she hated to swim, and I assumed that getting her head wet made her feel like she was drowning. It seemed that as her Alzheimer's progressed, her brain was losing connections. The fears embedded in her psyche from early on in life were still there, but now her brain couldn't differentiate between when she was safe and when she was not.

I quietly stepped backward into the bedroom. By that time, I knew that more people caused her more confusion. The caregivers were almost done, and the most important thing was that my mom was safe, and the water would be going over her face for only a minute. I went back to the office and kept working. At noon, I drove back to my house to fix lunch for me and Liam, then drove back to my mom's to complete paperwork and farm expenses in my office, before I picked up Hannah after school, took her to a soccer game, and finally went home in the late afternoon to prepare dinner.

After a while, I stopped asking Liam about getting a job. Him refusing to look for one was a tremendous weight on me, but each night when I crawled into bed, exhausted, and he held me tightly and whispered, "I love you" into my ear, I justified it all.

13

Disturbance

One evening in February, my mom had a tonic-clonic seizure. My dad called me around 7:30, and right away I drove over to their house. He and I had a hard time getting my mom up off the floor, and once we got her seated on the sofa, she fell over and had another seizure. I called 911, and stayed with her all night at the hospital. They had her hooked up to what seemed like hundreds of tiny magnets attached to wires all over her body. She was in a comatose state. It was a couple of days before she opened her eyes and recognized us.

The doctor told my dad and me that in order for my mom to live, she was going to need a feeding tube. "Do whatever it takes to keep her going," my dad said.

The night before my mom's operation, the surgeon who would be inserting the feeding tube called. He asked me poignant questions in regard to her care and state of being once a feeding tube was her only means of sustenance. I told him that these were not questions for me, but rather for my dad, her spouse. By this time in the progression of my mom's disease, I had come to the conclusion that the best way to handle her condition was to let my dad make the major decisions concerning her care. My mom and dad were here on this Earth before me, and had established their loving relationship before I was around. I was making minor decisions, but for the important ones, I defaulted to my dad. It's not that I couldn't make major decisions, but under the circumstances, I chose to honor his. My dad was determined and strong. He called the doctor back and told him to put that feeding tube in immediately, and that he didn't want to hear another word the doctor had to say. Like a reigning knight, my dad was going to fight for my mom's life until the very end.

I was at the hospital every day until we could bring my mom home. When we finally did, the main caregiver and I had to learn how to insert the bottles of liquid food into the lines without getting air in them, and when and how much to feed her. There was a whole new lineup of medications to learn how to administer. We also had to turn her often, so that she didn't get bedsores, and had to take extra care in keeping her skin dry. After a couple of days, my dad noticed that my mom's breathing was shallow; he called the doctor and told him that she needed oxygen. They sent over the tanks that afternoon. Each night when I got home, drained from caring for my mom, Hannah had made dinner. She was an angel.

My mom was on the feeding tube for about four weeks. I could feel the toll it was taking on my dad. One afternoon, when he was out irrigating and shoveling a big washout of holes from gophers, Liam went out to see him.

"Hey, Sam, why don't you let me help you here?" Liam said.

That was the moment my dad hired my husband to work for him. My dad would later say that Liam got him at a weak moment.

Liam didn't want to work for any money. He tried a couple of times to say that this was not why we were here in Patterson working on the farm, and he portrayed it as another example of what an altruistic person he was. I immediately thought: *I cannot continue to afford for him not to have a salary.* At the same time, something made me think to contact the attorney I had consulted during my divorce from Dale. When I called her, she told me that under no circumstances was Liam to work for nothing. By working without receiving payment, the lawyer explained, he could later take everything. For Liam to be an employee protected me and my parents in that regard. The lawyer surmised that Liam might already know this, and that was why he didn't want to take a salary or be paid on the books. I defended him, of course, believing what Liam told me to be true, and not what she surmised.

My dad left it up to me. I thought about it for a day or so, trying to figure out what Liam's salary should be. Then I had it. I told Liam he could have the same salary as me. *How nice,* I thought, *we each make the same amount. That's perfect.* It was adequate. Not big, but appropriate. I could tell he wasn't happy, but he had no rebuttal. Since I earned the same amount, what could he say? He sighed and accepted it.

Remarkably, my mom slowly recovered to the point that her feeding tube could be removed. It was very uncomfortable watching the doctor yank it out of her stomach. He was a wonderful doctor, and he came to my parents' home for visits. It was hard to find the old-fashioned kind of doctor that still made house calls. Whenever he came to check on my mom, she perked up. He was handsome and patient, and would assuredly hold her hand, looking at her and explaining things simply and well.

The removal of my mom's feeding tube felt like a milestone,

but I was sad that she never recovered beyond that. I missed the mom I knew, and I missed her companionship even more. She could no longer help us when we got her dressed. If I said, "Hold out your left foot, so I can put your sock on," she would hold out her right foot, or lift up her left arm. Then I would say, "No, not that one" or "Here, this one." It made no difference; she was losing her cognitive function. When my kids were little, and I was teaching them to hold out their left foot to put on a sock, maybe they didn't understand it right away, but the next day, and the day after that, they did. It was so exciting to feel that acquired learned experience with them. Now, with my mom, it was the exact opposite. With each of what at one time had been simple tasks, my mom was now de-acquiring learned experiences. I tried my best to remain cheerful with each direction or instruction, but sometimes it made me too sad, and I wanted to cry. But I didn't want to cry in front of my mom, because often she would start to cry and tell me she was so sorry, she didn't know what was happening to her, and that she felt afraid. "It's all okay, sometimes we just forget things," I would tell her. "And I'll be here to help you. I love you, Mom."

It was now springtime, and Liam was working with my dad. The first time I handed Liam his paycheck, he glanced at it, then looked up at me and said, "Hey, honey, are you going to the bank this afternoon?"

I was always going to the bank, so I said, "Yes," and asked him why.

"I'm helping your dad," he said slowly. "I'll never be able to get away before the bank closes. Since you're going, I'll give you a deposit slip," he said, and paused. "Do you think you could be so kind as to make the deposit for me?" It sounded like more of a statement than a question, but at the time it didn't really register. From that point on, Liam asked me to do this for every single paycheck, so along with the checks that I was still writing for his two mortgages, I was now depositing his paychecks as well.

When Liam first started working for my dad, he was congenial and easygoing. That first year, any question he asked me about the farm, I answered eagerly and felt enlivened. We were partners working together for the common goal: to keep the family farm going strong for the next generations.

In California, all farmers must complete a test in order to use spray materials for pesticides while operating a farm. My dad had always taken this test, but now that Liam was on board, he took over the responsibility. After Liam passed the test, I noticed a change in his attitude. With his newfound omniscience, he began to patronize me about the farm; there was no more asking me questions. Something about this seemed strange, almost as if I had been used for my knowledge, then dumped, and he didn't need my input or familiarity with the farm anymore.

The end of that year is when real trouble started between Liam and my dad. One day, when he came home for lunch, he looked at me with disdain and said, "What are you trying to do, throw me under the bus?"

"What are you talking about?" I said.

"You didn't tell me about that small, odd-sized piece of land in the center of the orchards. I'm out there trying to do the best I can, and it's as if you've tied one arm behind my back."

"I'm so sorry," I said. "I forgot about that piece. Let me draw you a map."

"I'd appreciate that," he said. "That way I don't have to keep bugging your dad and Arturo."

I already had a map, along with a few hand-drawn ones

of my dad's that showed the underground irrigation piping system that my grandpa had put in. I had these maps in my Almond Timeline, but thought I would draw a more specific one.

The next day, when I went to work in my office at the farm, I saw my dad in the kitchen. "Liam started disking the wrong fields," he said, shaking his head. "Unbelievable. He can't tell one orchard from another. Fortunately, I stopped him before he continued much further."

"I have to go do some work in the office," I said. I stood up from the kitchen table and left. As I was walking to my office, I realized that must have been the reason Liam had asked me for the map.

A couple of months later, Hannah's eighth grade class was going on a field trip to Washington, D.C., and other historical sites on the East Coast. They needed parents to chaperone, and so I volunteered. I had never been to Washington, D.C., before, and I was looking forward to seeing the capitol. The only reason I felt comfortable leaving was because my mom's status had not changed. Her decline was not accelerating at a rapid rate, nor had she had any recurring seizures since starting on her medication.

Hannah and I were on a bus with her classmates, teachers, and parents going from Delaware to Virginia when the phone calls from Liam and my dad started coming in. Liam must have called me five times within two hours, and my dad called just as many times. It was hard trying to figure out exactly what had happened. Each one was so upset that I couldn't follow what they were saying. The dispute had something to do with a chainsaw.

According to my dad, it was a really good chainsaw that

no one had ever broken, except for Liam. "He was wielding it around like he was King Kong," my dad said. "He was so damn hard on it, like he is on all the equipment." A few minutes later, Liam called and said, "Your dad's out of his mind. I didn't break any chainsaw, if that's what he's telling you. It's an ancient piece of crap that needs to be repaired, just like the rest of the junk here on this farm."

Liam also talked about how my dad had told him to disk one of the orchards. This particular orchard had not been pruned that year, and the lower branches were hanging down low in an arch. He called the trees "man killers" and claimed that my dad was trying to kill him by insisting that he disk that orchard. Liam was talking fast and vehemently, which was not his usual style, and it was so noisy on the bus that all I kept hearing was him repeating over and over that my dad was trying to kill him. Liam said that as he was disking, the branches just about knocked him off the tractor, and that suddenly, out of nowhere, one branch whipped around like a boomerang and hit the gearshift, causing the tractor to stop. He said he jammed it into reverse and was almost thrown off the tractor when it lurched forward. Another time, he said, he was ducking, moving left to right constantly, and his cap got scraped right off the top of his head, along with his sunglasses, which got disked beneath the tractor—thanks to my dad, he added.

But don't all the guys go out there and disk those fields? I thought.

I was across the country, and didn't want Liam to walk off the farm, nor did I want my dad to have a heart attack over this while I was gone. I felt sick. Everyone around me looked happy and carefree. Parents were laughing, pointing at historical monuments, telling stories, and some of the kids were singing patriotic songs. All of this was going on around me, while my husband and father were at war out in the fields in California. I couldn't do anything from that bus. I tried to console each one and tell them how I thought the other one must have meant something different from how it was being interpreted. I quickly learned not to add fuel to the fire, nor to disregard their point of view, nor sound as though I were defending the other one, because that only made things worse. I had to do damage control.

A few minutes later, my dad called again and said, "Don't listen to that guy, whatever he tells you. It's not the truth. The guy is not all there."

After I hung up with my dad, Liam called again. He claimed that my dad didn't have the correct tractors. "Correct tractors? What do you mean?" I asked as our bus with forty-something singing kids around me rumbled toward Mount Vernon, George Washington's home overlooking the Potomac River.

"They're not the right kind," was all Liam said.

"Not the right kind?" I said. "Well what kind are they, then? He's used that kind of tractor my whole life."

"They're big and heavy, for out in the open field," Liam said. "We need orchard tractors. Low-profile tractors that have tire fenders so a limb can't get tangled up in the tire, like what happened to me. You gotta get back here before your dad kills me."

As I was talking to Liam, I put him on hold because my dad was calling at the same time. "Liam is crazy," he said. "You gotta get back here and get this monkey off my back. He tried to kill me out in the field when he threw the chainsaw at me. It came within inches, flew right past me. You know, it was just me and him out there. I'm an old man. How could I have defended myself from that mean, deranged wrestler?"

I went back and forth with call waiting, putting one on hold, while I told the other I would call him back in a few minutes.

Later that day, after we left Mount Vernon, we visited the Library of Congress. In the gift shop, as I reached for an antique Woodmere Thomas Jefferson teacup, I was so distracted that I accidentally knocked it over; it went crashing to the floor, shattering loudly into tiny pieces. The store immediately became silent, parents turned around, and the shop staff came rushing over and looked at me. Embarrassed, I offered to pay for it, but the gift shop manager said that because our group had purchased quite a few things, it was okay.

In the mornings at breakfast, and in the evenings after dinner, parents would sit with one another and compare notes about the historical sites we had visited. At the last hotel, many of them had gone down to the lobby bar at night. I felt anti-social and could not seem to push myself out of myself. My brain could only hold so much, and it was at capacity. I stuck with buying books and reading them in the evening. One was about Ulysses S. Grant, and another was about Daniel E. Sickles, an interesting character in the Battle of Gettysburg.

In the book about Sickles, I read that in 1859 he had shot and killed his wife's lover, Philip Barton Key II, who happened to be the son of Francis Scott Key, who wrote "The Star-Spangled Banner." Sickles would become the first person to successfully use a defense of temporary insanity. It was a few years later that it dawned on me that the very book I had been reading on this trip would have an eerie similarity to my future. Sickles' treatment toward his wife has been likened to what is called gaslighting. Gaslighting is a form of psychological abuse, in which information is selectively omitted to favor the abuser, and things are twisted around so that the victim starts to doubt their own perception of reality. Slowly, Liam was gaslighting me; I just couldn't see it at the time.

One afternoon, our group toured the solemn area where the Battle of Gettysburg had taken place in July 1863. We looked at some of the cannons that remained and went over to the ridge of limestone rocks and peach orchards where Robert E. Lee's final assault, known as Pickett's Charge, had taken place. Peaches are such a sweet, delectable fruit, and to have one of the Civil War battles be fought out in the middle of a peach orchard seemed like quite an irony, let alone that it was peaches again... As I stood there on the knoll at Pickett's Charge, next to the rocks, and looked out, I thought it uncanny that my husband and my father were battling in orchards on the West Coast while I toured battlefields in orchards on the East Coast. I had to get home fast.

Unfortunately, there were still another couple of days of our trip remaining, so I had to ride it out. When I finally got back home to Patterson, both my dad and Liam had calmed down. They each gave me their version of events, and I pieced together what I believed had taken place. They'd gotten into a huge fight out in the field. My dad, standing at the rear of his pickup with the tailgate down, had said, "You know, Liam, I could have rented out this land to Brian Ellis." Brian was a good friend of my dad's and an excellent third-genera-tion farmer. In response, Liam had thrown the chainsaw into the back of the pickup, barely missing my dad, and said, "Go ahead, rent it out to Brian Ellis, I don't give a damn. Virginia and I will move to Tucson. Besides, we were only here to help you and Irene out, because of her Alzheimer's. This isn't where we wanted to be anyway." My dad held Liam's arm and pleaded with him. "Please don't go," he said. "Please let's try to get along for Virginia. Let's do this for her."

When Hannah and I returned from Washington, D.C., it was the summer between her eighth-grade year and her freshman year of high school. She would stay with me during the week, and I'd take her to tennis at different times of the day, depending on the coach and the tennis academy. No matter how late we came home, Liam was always up waiting patiently for us to eat dinner together. I'd grab takeout on the way home, or we'd eat the one-dish meal I had started early that morning in the slow cooker. Liam was my cornerstone. Hannah would spend the weekends with her dad and his third wife and her four daughters in Orinda.

When Dale enrolled Hannah in high school for the fall in Orinda without talking to me first, I was livid. He said that's where she was going because that was where he had gone, and there was no better school anywhere. I could never hold a conversation with him about the pros and cons, or exchange views on what might be the best environment for our daughter. It was always about Dale, and where he went, and what he did, and where he was born, and where he grew up, and where our children were born, and where they would live forever in Orinda. Dale constantly told me that I was the one who had moved; I had abandoned the children. He would often say, "You can hire people to do what you're doing," implying that my mom and dad didn't need my help. During the same conversation in which he told me he'd enrolled Hannah in high school in Orinda, he also said he was going to see to it that Hannah would never come back to live with me. Every conversation left me feeling disheartened.

In spite of Dale's relentless mantra about Orinda, and his unfounded accusations of abandonment, in my heart I hoped and prayed that one day the kids would understand why I had moved back to my parents' farm. With no siblings to share in the caregiving, I bore full responsibility for my parents' physical and financial wellbeing. I hoped that by my actions, my kids would see what it means to take care of your parents as they grow old, and the sacrifices and choices we are faced with in life.

I have always told my children that the only thing certain in life is change, and that when things are going well, we must cherish that time and remember it when things are not going well, because when things are not going well, they could be worse, or they could get better. We must never give up hope for a better day ahead, because circumstances inevitably change.

One evening that summer, Liam, Hannah, and I drove to our favorite frozen yogurt place in downtown Patterson. It was always busy, packed with kids, adults, and all ages in between. We walked by a waterfall fountain surrounded by flowers and plants, and on in to the yogurt shop, where we stood in the long line. Just as we reached the counter, after waiting for twenty minutes, my phone started to ring. It was my dad. Visibly annoyed, Liam and Hannah rolled their eyes, and Hannah started asking me what flavor I wanted. "Anything," I mouthed, trying to listen to what my dad was saying.

He was clearly upset. "Can you come over here right now?" he said. "I don't know what to do about Anna." Anna was one of the all-night caregivers for my mom, and a shift change was to have occurred at 7:00 p.m. At first, I thought maybe she hadn't shown up. She had always been so reliable, though, and I couldn't imagine her being a no-show.

Right then, Hannah and Liam started motioning at me with their hands to hang up the phone. They kept pretending like they were holding a phone and putting it down on the receiver. Liam was shaking his head. "Call him back," he kept repeating. "Why does he always have to call when we're together?"

"Some guy is on the run," my dad was saying, as I shifted my concentration back to the phone. My eyes darted back and forth between Hannah and Liam. "He must have stolen a car, or robbed a store or something. There are cops everywhere. On the ground and above the house." I turned my back to Liam and Hannah's annoying pantomimes, and walked out of the yogurt place. All I could understand from my dad was something about helicopters and police everywhere, and Anna fast asleep.

"I'll be right over," I told my dad.

I walked back into the yogurt shop and told Liam and Hannah that we had to go. Needless to say, they were not happy. They asked to be dropped off first at our house, not knowing how long I would be, which made sense, but when I got to our house, Hannah wanted to go with me, and Liam said he was staying home. He got out of the car, and I continued on with Hannah. When I turned down the road to my parents' house, I could see the blue lights of police cars flashing in several places. They stopped me and asked where I was going. I told them I was going to check on my parents. The cops said that if my parents had any dogs, they were to put them inside, or enclose them in some way, because they had policemen on foot with dog trackers out looking for a suspect. He also told me to leave the entry gate open.

I opened the electronic entry gate and drove down the long, paved driveway, then around to the side entrance of the house. Hannah and I went into the kitchen to see my dad and find out what was going on. He was sitting at the kitchen table, visibly distraught. "You couldn't believe this place," he said. "It was lit up like a Christmas tree. There were helicopters circling above, with searchlights and beacons lighting up the whole house. I've never seen anything like it. I went into the bedroom where mom is, and where Anna is, to *tell* Anna what was going on," he continued, "and to make sure the sliding glass door in the bedroom was closed and locked, and when I went in there, Anna was sound asleep. 'Hey Anna,' I hollered to her a coupla times from across the room. She didn't move, and I was afraid she wasn't even alive, so I went over and shook her on her shoulder; she woke up and jumped, saying that I had scared her. 'I scared *you?*' I said. 'You're scaring *me*, the fact that you're sound asleep.' "

She was supposed to be awake during the night to take care of my mom, turning her over and changing her, if needed. And how in the world could she sleep through all the commotion of a police chase surrounding the house? Anna apologized for falling asleep, explaining that she was in nursing school and up late studying on her days off from work. Things had settled down a little, and I saw that my dad was feeling more comfortable. He said he just wanted to go to bed and get some sleep. I told him what the police officer had said about the dog and the gate, then Hannah and I got into the car and started to drive back home. On the main street, I could hear the helicopters flying low above us by the deafening whooshing sound of the blades. I couldn't believe it: they were following my car. I got about a quarter of a mile down the two-lane highway when the police chopper blasted out of the loudspeaker, "The silver SUV, pull over to the right, immediately. I repeat, the silver SUV pull over to the right and stop your vehicle." I looked over at Hannah and told her not to be afraid. I could not believe the police were pulling us over. *They must think we're the bad guys and we stole this car,* I thought. Hannah and I were surrounded. Military-style flashlights were pointed right at our faces. It was hard to see and hear with the chopper hovering so low and loud above, and when three highway patrolmen opened all the car doors, the wind from the blades blew in. They asked me for my driver's license, where I was going, and where was I coming from. After inspecting the car, they told me I was free to go. I thought it would be too bad if I'd taken the heat off the actual suspect, and now he'd gotten away because they'd put their resources into going after me. Hannah and I made it home, although it gave Hannah's dad yet another reason to see to it that she attended school in Orinda.

As the summer became fall, and Hannah went back to school in Orinda, I missed her terribly. I missed both of my children. My sadness over Hannah's departure, combined with the mounting expenses that Liam was asking me to cover, made me anxious. Liam would constantly remind me of the successful career he'd given up in order to live on the farm, so that I could help my parents as my mom's disease progressed. "Can't you see how I've humbled myself to accept working with your dad?" he would often say.

For an instant, I thought, *Now, wait a second, here.* Weren't we supposed to be a team? Why was Liam suddenly talking as if he were the only one who had made a sacrifice? It felt contradictory to the "we" that had become so engrained in my head.

Feeling responsible for the sacrifice that Liam had me convinced he'd made, each month I continued to pay for his two mortgages, the caretaker and pruning of the trees at his house in Tucson, his son's education, and his daughter and son-in-law's trips out to visit us with their children. I liked having them over, and it made me feel like I was helping to bond Liam with his kids after the years of alienation. It also made me feel whole, as if I were part of that big family that I had always longed for.

In mid-fall came the harvest season. At lunchtime, when Liam would come home from the fields, instead of being inquisitive and asking how we did things on the farm, he would embed criticisms into his questions. He would tell me again about the farm that he grew up on with his Mormon foster parents in Illinois, and magnify their successes. They farmed a thousand acres and shared equipment, and things had run so smoothly, he said. I had no reason to doubt him, since I had seen the farm myself. One Fourth of July, before we were married, on the way to visit Liam's sister, we had driven by his family's farm. It had been sold to someone else, but as we drove by, Liam gave descriptions of the old barn and the ice house.

One day, Liam abruptly stated that he would no longer be drinking any alcohol. "Mormons don't drink, and I haven't been living by the standards I grew up with," he said. "That's fine with me," I told him. "I drank enough wine in my first marriage." After that, our pre-dinner ritual of having a glass of wine, eating cheese and crackers, and talking about the day no longer happened.

For Thanksgiving, Liam's daughter's family came to visit again. Hannah came for a day, and we all cooked in the kitchen, making hors d'oeuvres, pies, and homemade rolls. It was during these times that I thought for sure all was well, and all was as it was meant to be. I showed Liam's granddaughter how to crack nuts, carefully, just a few at a time.

Before dinner, my dad called to say he wasn't feeling well, and that he wouldn't be coming over for Thanksgiving. We all jumped in the car and went over there to see why, and after we told him that it just wouldn't be the same without him, my dad changed his mind.

One morning, my mom told me that her heart hurt. I didn't understand what she meant, but I figured she was trying to tell me that she felt sad. Stammering and pausing between words, she asked if Sam, my dad, was dead. It was distressing to see her so tormented by her own thoughts. When I was finally able to reassure her that my dad was alive and healthy, and that he loved her, my mom collapsed onto the floor and started crying. She was so happy to understand. Even though it was only five minutes of understanding, I felt a tremendous sense of relief seeing her recognize, if briefly, that he was alive.

On another day, when I got to her house, the caregivers were helping her as usual, and when she looked over at me, she thought I was her sister. "Oh, Charlotte, come over here, you're strong," she said. "Get these strangers out of my house. Hurry, I don't want them here, who are they? Why are they here? They're bothering me. Get them out." I sat down beside her, put my arm around her, and said, "They are the caregivers, and they're helping us." Her Alzheimer's disease kept methodically eroding her brain.

A couple of months later, my mom broke her hip and fell to the floor. It occurred to me that when she'd kept saying that her heart hurt, maybe she actually meant her hip. I'm sure her heart could have hurt, too, because the Alzheimer's was robbing her of her memory and her ability to relate to the man she loved so much, her husband.

The doctor ordered a mobile X-ray to find out what was going on. It turned out that she had a hip fracture. It was determined that had the fall caused her hip to break, she would have been badly bruised. By the hip essentially fracturing in one part, the doctors could see from the X-rays that the hip break had caused the fall, not the other way around. From there on out, my mom was completely bedridden and not long after, she got pneumonia from aspirating her food. No matter how careful we all were when it was our turn to feed her, somehow when she ate, food would go down her windpipe and into her lungs. From that she could not recover, and she slowly died.

It was Easter week when the caregiver called at 1:00 a.m. and told me that my mom's blood pressure was 64 over 44. I jumped out of bed, got dressed, and drove over to my parents' house. I was so glad that I lived only seven minutes away. As my mom slipped away during the early morning hours, the caregiver and I listened to a CD that my mom's best friend, Eleanor, had brought over the week prior, along with a CD player. The CD was titled *Something Beautiful*, and it featured Southern gospel medleys by Bill and Gloria Gaither. It sounded exactly as its title indicated. The songs were uplifting melodies with lyrics of faith and hope, and as my mom slipped away, it was truly moving to hear. At one point, the CD player happened to seemingly randomly get stuck on one song, and it kept repeating it over and over. The music sounded like an orchestra with solo parts of piano, then flute. Their voices were in harmony, and sounded like angels rejoicing, calling my mom home. After twelve hours, she passed.

Several months earlier, when I was tucking my mom into bed, she'd looked up at me and said, "You take good care of Liam. He's a good man." It was one of the last coherent things she said to me, and I took it to heart.

Before the funeral, Liam told me that the few suits he owned he'd left in Tucson. He was now a farmer, he said, and he didn't need them anymore. When he lived in Alamo and worked as a sales manager, he explained, he'd had many more, but they'd been eaten by moths, and he had to give them away. So when my mom died, we went to a men's custom tailor shop, and I bought Liam a tobacco-colored, windowpane plaid double-breasted suit; Allen Edmonds shoes; a belt; shirts; and ties.

For my mom's funeral, my dad chose a golden rose stainless steel eighteen-gauge casket with a light pink velvet interior, and a raised image of Jesus carrying the cross on each of its four corners. Right away, it made me think of the cross that was my mom's Alzheimer's disease. Looking at the casket also made me think of how each one of us has our own cross to bear. Life is not perfect, and as I see it, it's about how we carry our crosses; often, the crosses we bear can be the result of other people's crosses. Do we complain about them? Do we suffer in silence? Or a little of both? During trying times in my life, I would mentally search for a meaning to my suffering, and the choices I had made, and I would ask myself, *Why?*

For twenty years, my mom and dad had vacationed in Hawaii. My mom loved Hawaiian music, and so for the service, I chose two of her favorite songs. "Beyond the Reef" played as the service began, and "Beyond the Blue" played as people paid their respects and viewed her in the open casket. At the cemetery where we gathered for the burial, Liam said a short prayer that he told me he'd recited as an elder in the Mormon Church. At the time, I felt thankful to be married to such a religious person, and as he quoted scripture, I thought to myself, *This is one of the many reasons I love him.*

14

Thunder

As spring turned into summer, Liam and my dad continued to argue about how to do each job. One wanted to disk the weeds, one wanted to spray the weeds and mow. One day, my dad called to tell me that Liam would be home for lunch, and that Arturo would be running the sprayer for him over the lunch hour. It seemed like a strange reason for my dad to call because Liam was always home for lunch, anyway. In fact, fifteen minutes later, Liam walked through the door and said, "No one will be spraying today. We ran out of herbicide."

"Wait, what?" I said. "My dad just called and told me that Arturo would be running the sprayer."

"I don't know why he told you that. Arturo was eating his lunch, and your dad was right there."

I did not understand what was going on. They were all down there together, but it seemed that more and more, I was getting conflicting accounts of what was happening on the farm. It was just like with the Schmeiser. The Schmeiser

V-blade was a piece of land-leveling equipment used to knock down high spots of dirt to fill in the low spots; namely, ruts caused by tire tractors or harvest debris. Liam told me that we absolutely needed a Schmeiser V-blade for the orchards to level the dirt. Every time he said this, all I kept thinking was how my dad would fly through the roof if we bought a new piece of equipment without consulting him first. I grew up listening to story after story of this person and that person who blew through their inheritance and lost the family farm by thinking they could run the business better than their predecessors.

With my mom gone, and his siblings and parents also departed, my dad had no one but me to share his love of the land with. I understood how hard he'd worked for it, what he'd done to better the farm, and how hard my mom had worked to help him. They were the A-Team in my eyes. My dad knew when to "cut across the field," as he called cutting corners, and when not to. Over the course of my mom's illness and eventual death, I learned so much more about my dad than I ever really knew, or could see at the depths that I was able to see during those later years. So when Liam kept talking about how "we" needed to buy this Schmeiser V-blade grader thing, I kept holding off on a decision. "Let's just wait a while," I told him. Liam ultimately became so adamant about having this piece of equipment that he went to one of the companies where we had an account and ordered an eight-foot Schmeiser for $5,000. I felt intense anxiety, as if I were lying to my dad, because this was still his farm, and that Schmeiser was not a small tool. Out of respect for my dad, who was actually the manager of the farm, Liam should have consulted him first.

In that moment, I felt as though I were being tested. *What was my duty? What was my moral commitment?* I asked myself. Should I take my husband's point of view? After all, the Bible says to leave your mother and father, and you and your spouse shall become one union. *Does that mean I should support and back up Liam?* I wondered, even though he'd tried to persuade me that my dad was old and feeble and could no longer make good decisions. Or should I stand by my dad, who had been at the helm for fifty years? I was at a disadvantage when it came to knowing what was really going on out in the fields.

Whenever I carried out financial transactions at my dad's home office, or the accountant's office, or the lawyer's office, it seemed to me that my dad was exceptionally competent. I was torn over what to do. I hated the fact that I had been divorced once before, and I wanted to do the right thing in this second marriage. I didn't want to make any more mistakes. So I looked at the Bible as my relationship manual, and I made the decision to follow what it said, and to unite with my husband.

After Liam picked up the Schmeiser and took it down to the field, my cell phone started ringing. First it was Liam, then my dad, then Liam again, then my dad again. My dad was practically hyperventilating. "What the hell is going on?" he said, infuriated. "The guy is crazy buying a stupid thing like that. It's too small. No one uses that size. It's worthless. It's a piece of shit. The guy is a boneheaded idiot. I'm calling Joe down there at the tractor place to see if we can return it right now and get the money back. How much did you pay for that? I know you bought it. I know you did."

Liam and my dad were on the warpath again, and each was dragging me along with him.

The second I hung up with my dad, Liam called me, seething. "If your dad calls and tells you to return the Schmeiser, you tell him I said *NO*," Liam barked. "I already told him that this is *my* piece of equipment, and that I bought it. It's mine, and he can't take back something that's not his. It's mine."

The second I hung up with Liam, my dad called again. He had just gotten off the phone with Joe at the tractor place, and

Joe had told him that they could not take it back into inventory, because no one buys an eight-footer. They sell a lot of the ten-, eleven-, and twelve-footers, Joe said, and back in the Midwest, the potato farmers buy twenty- and thirty-footers. But the eight-foot ones are so small that there is hardly a market for them. My dad was livid.

Liam assured me that there were a lot of uses for the eight-footer out in the field. In fact, when he got home that evening, he told me about the spots where he'd used it. I cringed the next day when my dad called to tell me that Liam had made a few passes with the Schmeiser and made a huge hole, which Arturo was going to have to fill in with a different tractor and scraper.

That evening, when Liam came home, he said, "In case your dad tells you differently, I did a great job. I took the Schmeiser out, and knocked down the high spots and filled in the low spots. I don't think your dad even went out into the field to look at what I'd done. He's listening to Arturo, who didn't tell him the truth."

It was hard for me to sort out truth from fiction.

A month or two later, Liam and I went to see his daughter in Utah. In the hotel room the first evening, after unloading the luggage and getting settled, Liam pulled out the computer and started typing away. I asked him what was he doing that was so important. We had talked about going to get something to eat after we checked into our room.

"I'm documenting something," Liam said.

"Documenting something? What does that mean?" I asked.

"I'm recording the time that your dad tried to kill me," Liam said. "We'll go grab something to eat as soon as I'm done."

Oh, brother, I thought to myself, *this does not sound good.* A disgruntled employee who happened to be my husband suing a family member who happened to be my dad was the last thing I needed. Once again, I didn't like this situation. The only reason for someone to document an incident was if they planned to use it for some specific purpose, and I had a feeling that Liam was not doing it for benevolent reasons. I had a feeling his motives were baleful.

Each quarter of school that came, I continued to pay for Regan's college tuition and books, the two mortgages, Liam's dental, medical, and car insurance, and all other personal expenses. One time Liam asked for money to send to a private charitable organization that he had donated to in years past. I felt bad at the time asking him if we could wait on that a bit, as the finances were whittling away, and I was starting to have to dip into my own children's college fund just to pay for *his* children's college.

Liam got defiant and said, "Don't we have a trust fund somewhere from when your mom died?"

"No," I said quickly. "What my mom had when she died went to my dad, and rightly so. That's how they set it up."

His remark troubled me, and made me feel protective of my parents and everything they had worked for. I couldn't keep from wondering how long he had been thinking about that, and why. Also, for the first time ever, the "we" didn't sound good. Usually, I loved to hear Liam say "we," but this time, when he said, "Don't *we* have a trust fund somewhere from your mom?" it felt different.

By now, I was consumed with worry about money almost every day. I did not want to go bankrupt, then look back and think: I lost it all in the name of love.

Another time, when I brought up to Liam the fact that my

finances were really going fast, he said, businesslike, "Take out a loan against the house. Just go to your banker, they'll help you." Oh, yeah, right, I thought.

"Liam," I said. "There is no way I am taking out a loan against the house or the land, or anything."

He was missing my point entirely.

With my mom gone, and Hannah no longer living with me, since she was back in Orinda for the ninth grade, it felt like Liam was all I had. He had become my sole emotional support, as I had become his sole financial support. But at what price?

During cold winter nights, he warmed up my side of the bed before I crawled in beside him. I would feel his arms wrap around me, and hear him whispering into my ear, his voice as smooth as honey, telling me that he loved me and was never going to leave me. It was these moments that lifted the heaviness in my heart, made my worries go away, and gave credence to what I thought was true love.

A few months later, I overheard Liam talking to his buddy Barry on iChat. Barry was asking him a question about his medical insurance. Liam said, "I don't know, Virginia takes care of all that." Then I heard Barry say, "Oh, man, wow, will she take care of me, too?" I was just starting to walk into the office when I caught the expression on Liam's face. It was a smug kind of half smile. Something about it bothered me, although I was so emotionally dependent on him by that point that I still couldn't imagine my life without him.

My son, Cody, who was in eleventh grade, hardly ever came to visit. When Liam and I first got married, Cody didn't yet have his driver's license, and Dale would not bring him over to Patterson. The only time Cody came over is if I drove the hour-and-a-half to pick him up, took him back to Patterson with me, then brought him back to his dad's in Orinda. Dale told me that he would tell Cody that he ought to go see his mother, but at the same time, he wouldn't bring him over. Not even on Mother's Day. One Mother's Day, when Dale was married to his third wife, he called and said he'd told Cody that he was going to spend Mother's Day with his new mother, and that he wouldn't be going to Patterson to see me. I was furious. I loved my son. I was finally able to persuade Dale to allow Cody to be with me on Mother's Day.

Things between Liam and Cody had never been easy. The first year we were married, Liam and I took my kids to Hawaii. I paid for the trip, given that Liam had recently quit his job and wasn't working. Some of my friends from college were there with their families, too. The second day we were in Hawaii, Liam and Cody got into a huge fight. I couldn't figure out what had happened. All I could decipher was that Liam was telling Cody to return some towels to the pool attendant, they started yelling at one another, and then they all ended up *in* the pool: Cody, Liam, and the towels.

From that point on, Liam, who had previously encouraged me to keep a close relationship with my son, began discouraging me instead. One time, when I was getting ready to go see Cody at a swim meet, Liam told me that I was hovering too much. Another time, when I was on my way to a water polo match, Liam told me to "quit following him around." My son, at the time, was sixteen years old. If I expressed any concern over Cody, Liam would start to shake his head, as if to nonverbally communicate that he didn't want to hear it. "Cut the apron strings," he would say. His comments went against my own maternal instincts.

Finally when I managed to get to one of Cody's swim meets, he and I grabbed a bite to eat afterward, just the two of us. As we were talking, he asked, "Mom, why did Liam just up and quit his job and give up a high-paying salary to go and work on a farm?" Feeling defensive, I explained at length how Liam and I were going to take care of the farm and preserve it for generations to come. "Mom, really?" Cody said. "Think about it." My son was on to him, but I had no idea. I had blinders on.

15

Lightning

Four months after my mom died, Eleanor, her best friend, told my dad about a lovely lady who had just lost her grown son to the H1N1 flu virus in the same month that my mom had died. Her name was Charlotte, just like my mom's sister, and she was the same age as my mom. When my mom was still alive and lucid, she had told my dad that she wanted him to find a girlfriend after she died. She didn't want him to be alone.

One day, when I was working at the office at my dad's, he was trying to call Charlotte for the first time, and he said that he was having a problem with the phone number. Thinking it might be the wrong number, he told me to call Eleanor and get the number again. I did, and confirmed it was not a wrong number. I went back to the office and tried to continue working. My dad came into the office and said that he had just tried the number again, and that a man had answered, so he hung up.

"What?" I said.

"Yeah, that's it," my dad said, sounding glum. "I think it was a man that answered, and I'm not calling again."

"Let me see the number," I said, a bit baffled. "Maybe you dialed it wrong."

I dialed and right away, after one ring, Charlotte answered. I introduced myself and then, with a smile on my face, handed the phone to my dad.

At the time, Charlotte was living in Washington State to be near her daughter and grandchildren. She'd been born and raised in Patterson and had gone to the same high school as my dad, but since they were four years apart, they had never met. They spoke on the phone every day for twenty-one days without ever meeting in person. Then Charlotte came to visit. On the day she arrived, Hannah and I went over to my dad's house to welcome her. She drove in down the long, one-lane driveway in her white BMW sedan, with a couple of suitcases in the backseat. She got out of the car, met my dad, and after he showed her around the house, they paused and looked at each other.

"Should I get my bags?" she asked.

"Yes, let's go get them right now," my dad said.

My mouth just about dropped to my knees.

Charlotte moved in for good that very day. At first, I wasn't thrilled. I was upset by how fast things were moving. My mom had been gone only four months, and the week before Charlotte arrived, my dad told me that I had to remove all of my mom's belongings and take them over to my house. That meant every single item, he emphasized. I made trip after trip with all of my mom's clothes, photo albums, and keepsakes. This was tiring, both emotionally and physically. When someone dropped by to visit, they would ask me if we were moving because there were so many boxes stacked up everywhere.

The day after Charlotte moved in, my dad called and thanked me for removing my mom's things. He said he knew it was hard, but that he and Charlotte had told each other that since they didn't have a lot of time left in life, if they liked each other, they wanted to enjoy what time they did have left.

Even though I was still mourning my mom's death, Charlotte was loving and kind, and it was obvious how much she liked my dad. I could see that they were both happy, and each seemed to be walking on air. They had undeniable chemistry. They even had the same facial structure and tall, thin body type. They had some ups and downs, but within a few months' time, they had straightened it out. From then on, my dad and Charlotte seemed happy.

Charlotte had such a positive impact on my dad. For example, I had been trying for several years to get him to wear a hearing aid. When Charlotte came to live with him, I noticed that she wore one of those fancy, high-tech hearing aids that was so small it was almost invisible. One day, when they went out shopping together, my dad bought one, just like that, as quick as could be, with no fuss. What a difference Charlotte made in his life.

As my wariness toward Charlotte wore off, Liam's wariness increased, and eventually turned to anger. At the same time, she was no fan of his, either. I didn't recognize it at the time, but I later came to understand that Charlotte posed an existential threat to Liam's long-term plan. If Charlotte and my dad were to marry, she could have derailed the future of the farm. And Liam, as I would soon come to know, had his own designs on my family's land.

Later that same year, my dad and Charlotte planned a trip

to Bainbridge Island so he could meet her family. Liam and I were included in this plan, even though Liam grumbled about it, and was noticeably perturbed. It was apparent to me that if he flatly said he wasn't going, it would cause even more discord. To me, it seemed like a fun weekend trip.

On a Monday, four days before we were scheduled to leave, my dad came over to visit by himself. He talked about Liam for half an hour. "The guy is tearing up the equipment," my dad said. "He doesn't want to irrigate or spray during the night, and he spent an extra day going over one section of almonds to be raked before harvest, driving the rake back and forth, back and forth, getting every damn nut out there. There's a lot of work to do at harvest, and time can't be spent going over and over the same ground. I told him the orchard floor doesn't have to look like a tablecloth. It's a waste of time, energy, fuel, and money to pick up every single nut." My dad was becoming increasingly upset as he went on. "The guy has no common sense," my dad said. "There's something wrong with him. I'm telling you, he's just not right. And I don't want him to chase off Arturo, who we've had for ten years. Arturo can weld, and he knows every inch of this ranch. He has worked so hard. And now, for him to have to work alongside some lazy white fat butt who's fuckin' up all the time, I'm afraid we might lose Arturo. Then if we lose Arturo," my dad went on, "you might as well rent out the land, because the guy you married and brought home to the farm will lose it all."

Then my dad looked at me and pleaded. "I know you don't want to hear these things, Virginia, but you need to know what's going on."

I didn't say anything other than, "Wow, it's hard to believe that he would do that." So often I couldn't even speak. It was always so much to take in at one time. I loved and respected my dad, and at the same time, I was so in love with Liam. The constant tension between the two of them was wearing me down and wearing me out. I felt a heaviness in my chest that was increasing, little by little, day by day. I wanted them both to get along. I wanted so badly for our dream of farming to work out.

A few hours later, when Liam got home, he started in again on how my dad was losing it. "Your dad left so many nuts out there in the field that the guy driving the harvester pickup machine had to stop several times and climb down off of it. He raked the nuts by hand to get them into the windrow so the machine could get them all, then he climbed back up on the machine, and a few minutes later he would have to stop again and do the same thing. He finally came over and told me that we had to sweep those rows again. There were just too many nuts left behind. I had to redo some rows that your dad had done. Your dad shouldn't be out there in the orchards. He's too old, his mind is slipping, and he keeps messin' up and causing extra work for everybody. And he's getting worse."

I didn't say anything then, either, other than, "Wow, I can't believe my dad didn't see all the nuts he missed." I didn't tell Liam that my dad had been over a few hours before, nor did I share with him what my dad had told me.

I had to leave to pick up Hannah at tennis practice, then come back to make dinner and do the laundry. While my rote, everyday chores usually gave me a sense of normality, the increasing dissension between my dad and Liam was taking a toll on me.

The next morning, I woke up with one of the worst migraines I had ever had. My arms were limp and floppy like a ragdoll's. My head was pounding so hard that it was hard to see. I had to pull the curtains shut in the bedroom because the light from the window felt like stadium lights on a football field. I asked Liam to please whisper, because even though I knew he wasn't talking loudly, it sounded like he was screaming into a mega-phone right in my ears. I threw up. I couldn't sit. I couldn't lie down. It was awful. I called Kaiser and they told me to go to the emergency room. Liam drove me, and I cried in the emergency room when the nurse gave me pain medication. I think I cried because my head hurt so much, but also because I felt so grateful and relieved that someone was helping me and taking care of my needs.

Two days before we were scheduled to leave for Bainbridge Island, Liam announced that we were not going. He said that he didn't want to be traveling with me if I got another migraine. He was adamant. I still wanted to go, but wasn't about to pursue it. I wasn't sure if this was the hole that Liam had been looking for to get out of going.

When my dad would call from Charlotte's place, he'd describe the view from her balcony looking out over Puget Sound. In the evenings, they would sip cocktails and watch ocean liners and cruise ships pass by. Liam didn't want to hear anything about it, and he would cut me off by changing the subject whenever I started to tell him about my dad and Charlotte's trip.

The next year was more of the same. Each day I worried about money, and wondered how I was going to continue to pay for all of our household expenses, plus Liam's two mortgages, and his grown children's expenses. I also worried about the constant flare-ups between Liam and my dad. I would bring up the subject of Liam finding another job, and he would always hurl back at me, "Absolutely not, this is what we agreed to." But each night I spent at home with Liam would erase all the worry, as if someone had pushed the reset button.

One night, over dinner celebrating our four-year anniversary, he said out of left field, "Well, baby, we surpassed both my second and third marriages, pretty soon we'll be at ten years." On the one hand, this sounded positive, but on the other hand, it sounded like a challenge. It seemed strange to me that he had jumped straight up to ten years, as if that were a marker. *Why not six years,* I asked myself, because six would have been the marker that tied with his first marriage, if someone really wanted to keep track. It was another one of those moments that gave me pause, but as usual, when it came to Liam, I let my feelings veto my better instincts.

Little by little, Liam's easygoing disposition would falter when it came to my dad and the farm, like a small snowball gently rolling down the slope, getting bigger and bigger as it gains speed. One day, Liam came storming into the house for lunch. Usually it was a peaceful time, when we would chat about the morning, but this time was not like that. Pounding his feet as he walked down the hall from the garage, Liam bellowed, "When's the old man going to give up the ship?" He repeated it again as he walked into the kitchen, where I was making sandwiches. "I can run these ranches by myself," he said, waving his hand through the air in a grandiose manner. He puffed out his chest, threw his shoulders back, and continued, "Your dad keeps saying how he ran all this by himself. Right now, I can run this place by myself and do a better job than he ever did."

I was stunned. "Really?" I said, as I put our lunch on the table. "You could?"

"Yes," he said. "I've told you before. When I accepted your dad's offer to work here, I humbled myself down and sacrificed a high-paying salary. You wouldn't be worried about money if I'd kept my job and we were living in Tucson."

It was hard to admit to myself, but I was actually starting to get a little tired of him putting my family down, and his remarks were sounding clichéd. Now his repeated comments that he was "humbling himself down" sounded like a self-proclamation of automatic entitlement.

Now wait a minute, I thought, *sacrifice a job?* There he was talking about his sacrifice again. Liam and I had jointly agreed that we wanted to farm together, so how was that humbling himself down? I knew he was good, but was he that good? During this time, I started to have feelings of déjà vu. Was I going to have to choose between my husband and my dad? *No,* I thought, *that's crazy. Impossible.* It was a fleeting thought, and I shoved it to the back of my mind.

Another day, Liam said out of the blue, "We're going to have to get a guardianship for your father."

"A guardianship?" I repeated. "My dad doesn't need a guardianship. I have power of attorney, if he were to get sick. Gosh, Liam, I think my dad is just fine. I really do."

Liam let it go, but I had a strange feeling, almost as if he had been testing me and my reaction. I was not about to put my father away, or take away what few goals and daily activities he could do on his own out in the field. Once again, I had that strange fleeting thought... Oh, how I hoped I wouldn't have to choose between my husband and my father.

One afternoon in late May, as I started to make lunch, I was standing at the kitchen sink, looking out into the backyard. My thoughts were always, *Liam this* and *Liam that,* take out this loan, or move money from one account to another to cover for this or that expense. Up until this point in time, I'd believed that because I was so in love with Liam, I had to figure out all the ways I could make it work. But all of a sudden, as I stared out the window, I could see my thoughts as wooden boxes filled with water on a track heading down a mountain, like a train, picking up speed as they barreled toward a cliff. Then the wooden boxes of water turned into wooden buckets of water just before they went over a cogwheel, and right over the cliff. The minute the buckets of water went over that cliff, there was no stopping what happened next. I had a completely new way of thinking, as if I had entered an entirely different physical plane of existence, and I no longer thought about my troubles from my old perspective.

Right then, I knew that I had to get out of my relationship with Liam, and the only way to do that would be to divorce him. At that moment, an intense feeling of exhaustion and dread came over me, like a premonition of what was to come. It was as if I could see myself from the outside for the first time. In hindsight, I believe that what I had was an epiphany; it truly was a moment of revelation and insight.

Even though the shift helped to dislodge some of my steadfast ways of thinking, it still didn't stick. I kept asking myself if it was divine assistance, or the workings of Satan trying to push me toward another divorce. I felt deeply torn and conflicted.

16

Black Ice

It was now June. Daily life went on as normal, and on the surface, nothing had changed, but I kept waiting for the other shoe to drop. In the meantime, Liam had been developing a small lump just under his jawline. It was tiny at first, but we both observed that it had become noticeable in a relatively short period of time. An ear, nose, and throat specialist confirmed the lump was a common benign salivary gland tumor. If left alone for ten or more years, it had the capacity to grow into something malignant, so we decided it was best to take it out.

Liam made the appointment for July. Even through these doctor's appointments, I knew in the back of my mind that our marriage was going to end. It was as if I were in a play, and I was watching myself act. I was both in the audience and in the play at the same time. I didn't know what my next lines were, but they came out of my mouth as if I did.

A few days before his surgery, Liam called the painter, who

was a fellow Mormon, to ask for a blessing. One evening we drove over to the painter's house. On the way there, I felt crippled by intense anxiety. Of course, I wanted the surgery to go well, and of course I thought it was a wonderful thing to have a blessing before the surgery, but the thought of Liam not working while he was recovering scared me. What if he strung out the recovery for an indefinite period of time? The thought of continuing to be the sole provider *and* looking after my dad, and my daughter, and the farm, *and* caring for Liam for the next few weeks was beginning to feel like more than I could manage.

My dad had already told me that I had better not be paying Liam while he wasn't working. I didn't tell my dad that I couldn't afford *not* to pay him while he was off. I also had a strange feeling that with Liam, I had better pay him. He was recording things while he was working, and I wanted to protect my dad from any potential liability. Liam had sued his previous employer, so I knew what he was capable of. That lawsuit seemed to drag on and on. In the beginning of our marriage, I frequently asked Liam about it, but his answer was always the same: "I don't know. My attorney is working on it." Eventually, I stopped asking, just as I had stopped asking him about finding a job. What I really hoped was that if he received the lump sum, he wouldn't need to keep asking me to cover his expenses all the time.

The day before Liam's surgery, we went to the Mormon Church, which is officially known as the Church of Jesus Christ of Latter-Day Saints. I had never been to a Mormon service before. I was raised Catholic and didn't know anything about the Church of Latter-Day Saints. I had driven by a Mormon church in Patterson at least a hundred times, but I had never known exactly what it was; it resembled a church, with a pointy thing at the very top of the steeple, but the slim gold lettering for "The Church of Jesus Christ of Latter-Day Saints" was almost impossible to read against the red brick building.

As we were getting dressed to leave, Liam pulled out some all-white undergarments. I noticed that he had brought back a whole drawerful of them from his last trip to Tucson. The fabric was thin and silky, and the tops were a short-sleeved T-shirt style, while the trunks were short and fitted. Liam told me they were what he wore under his clothes while he was a practicing Mormon, and when attending Sunday service. "They're called temple garments," he said, "and if you and I start practicing and living by the Mormon way of life, you'll also be wearing these. They have them for the sisters, too."

When I asked more about the temple garments, Liam seemed hesitant to tell me, and also a bit irritated. "They are sacred, and are not to touch the floor, or any other clothing item in the drawers," he said. "They're white as a sign of purity, and when we wear them, we are reminded of keeping chaste, because they cover our private parts. It brings an awareness of sexual purity."

As Liam finished putting them on, I watched him out of the corner of my eye and wondered what he meant by the Mormon way of life. I didn't want him to see me looking at him and get even more irritated than he already was.

When we got to the Mormon church, we held hands down a long corridor and walked into a room with rows of padded banquet chairs. The room was divided into three sections. We went over to the right section and sat down. Liam proudly said that all the buildings are similar inside, and that most are modest and simple places. He said it as if "modest and simple" was indicative of high moral standards. I liked that.

A man in a dark suit stood at the podium and led the service. Liam called him a bishop. When it came time for what I had known as Holy Communion, young men in white shirts and black pants passed trays with bread and water down each row. Everyone else stayed seated and took a piece of bread and a sip of water from small plastic cups. The bread looked like big chunks of doughy French bread for fondue. I have celiac disease and cannot eat anything that contains gluten, especially wheat or bread. So when the bread passed by me, I said, "No, thank you." For the first time since my recent diagnosis, I was actually glad to have an excuse not to eat bread. The process of what the Mormons called "emblems of the sacrament" was strange to me. It didn't seem that holy or sacred.

Once we got home, I said to Liam, "Next week, let's go to the Catholic church. I miss it. Will you go there with me?"

"I am not going to the Catholic church, or any other church," Liam said sternly.

"Why? I went with you to the Mormon church. Why can't you go with me to where I grew up going?"

"Because my church does not allow it," he said gravely. "And I am not stepping foot in the Catholic church, or any other church, like I just told you. I'm not going." With that, he walked out of the room.

After that conversation, I concluded that it was either I go to the Mormon church with Liam, or go alone again to the Catholic church. In my first marriage, it had been hard to get my husband and my kids to go to church with me, so when Liam said he wouldn't go to a Catholic service, I was still glad that at least I had someone to go to *a* church with, even if it wasn't my familiar place.

The surgery was at 6:00 a.m. the next morning. I paid the $1,444 co-pay, winced at the cost, and subsequently got mad at myself for feeling that way. *What's the matter with me?* I thought. *What's happening?* It was unusual for me not to feel compassion, especially for a loved one right before a surgery.

But in this case, I felt like my funds were not just bleeding, now they were hemorrhaging.

The surgery went well, the doctor said, and the tumor was benign, just as he'd thought. It happened to be a sweltering day, with close to record highs in the triple digits. The nurses wheeled Liam out of the building as I ran to get the car. His face was bandaged up on one side and covered with black-and-blue bruises on the other; they'd wrapped the bandage from his chin, anchoring it up around the top of his head. As I pulled the car up, the heat waves were rising up off the cement. Maybe it was the way heat waves can make things look a bit distorted, like an optical illusion, or maybe it was because I was so hot and feeling so emotionally drained and financially burdened, but seeing Liam as he sat in the wheelchair with the nurse standing behind him, he looked like a bit of a monster.

When we got home, Liam said he was in a lot of pain and wanted some pills. He took two pain pills, then threw them up, along with the milkshake he had just drunk. Fortunately, the nurse had given us quite a stack of the blue barf bags, which Liam carried around for the next couple of days.

At night I slept in the bedroom while Liam sat propped up on the sofa in the living room. One night I woke up and thought I'd go see how he was doing. I started tiptoeing into the living room, when Liam growled in the dark, "What are you doing tiptoeing around like that? Where are you going?"

I hadn't seen that he was sitting straight up on the sofa, in the pitch-black room, and it startled me so much that I jumped a couple of inches off the floor, then slid across the tiles, my arms shot out on each side, and ran smack into a barstool. Regaining my balance, I said, "I was coming to check and see how you are, and if you need anything. I was trying to be quiet so I wouldn't wake you up if you were asleep."

"Yeah, right," Liam said. "You were sneaking around."

No, I thought to myself, *that is not what I was doing.* In the dark, shadowy night, Liam looked like a bit of a monster again. "I was coming to check on you," I repeated.

A few days later, he said, "Tell me now, what were you doing sneaking around in the middle of the night?" No matter how many times I told Liam that I was not sneaking around, that I was being careful not to wake him while I checked on him, it did not matter. He had glommed onto what he thought was his truth, and not what I was telling him, which was my truth.

One night, as we were sitting on the sofa, watching TV, he unexpectedly said, "When Hannah graduates next year, we can move to Tucson."

"I can't do that," I said, incredulous.

"That's what we talked about before we got married," he snapped back.

I sat there, quietly bewildered, shaking my head. "I don't think I said that."

"Had I known that you wouldn't move to Tucson," he said offhandedly. "I never would have married you."

In an instant I felt dejected.

A few days later, Liam told me he'd accepted that we would operate out of Patterson, but that we would travel back and forth to a warmer climate when it was cold in Northern California. I thought this sounded awful. We didn't live in Alaska, and we weren't some jet-setters chasing good weather around the country. The argument added to my already continuous ruminations about our situation, and Liam's comment about "never marrying me had he known" couldn't be taken back out of my psyche.

The next Sunday, we went to the Mormon church for the second time. This time a layperson, a woman in her late twenties, gave a fifteen-minute talk that sounded like a motivational speech. Another lady played the organ and sang a song, and the bread and water, of course, got passed around. I fell deep into contemplative thought about the fact that I couldn't reconcile my love for Liam with the strange predicament in which I'd found myself.

Three weeks had passed since Liam's surgery. The doctor had already cleared him the week before. He was healing fine and could resume work and his regular activities, but Liam didn't want to go back to work. His daughter, Sherrie, and her husband and their two children all flew out from Utah. It had been arranged a few months back that Liam and I would take care of the grandchildren while Sherrie and Dan went on vacation to the Bahamas. This was their fourth or fifth visit. Each time they came, they would sleep in Cody's room, which had a twin sofa sleeper for their daughter, Colleen, and I had bought a Graco Pack 'n Play for their one-and-a-half-year-old son, Danny.

Right before their visits, Liam would go into Cody and Hannah's bedrooms and take down the small hand-painted wooden crosses that I had put up on the wall next to each of their beds. Once, when I asked Liam why he'd done that, he answered, "We believe that it is a sin to have the instrument of Jesus's death displayed." At the time, it made me feel terrible, because I had never considered the idea that it would be a sin to display a cross. It sounded horrible; I couldn't believe that I had lived all those years without knowing this doctrine. Prior to that, I'd taken everything Liam told me to be true; he spoke with such authority on such a wide range of subjects that I always believed his explanations. This was the first time that one of them had given me pause.

The Sunday before Sherrie and Dan left for the Bahamas, we all went to the Mormon church together. This was now my third time, and I knew the drill. Liam put on his silky white temple garments under his suit, while I wore a dress and stockings and low pumps. This time, though, I started asking more questions—a *lot* more—and paying greater attention to the environment.

In the car on the way there, I learned the Mormon terminology. Each house of worship is called not a church but a meetinghouse, and the Sunday service is called a sacrament meeting. A temple is not open to the public; it is a building designated for members and only those members who are considered worthy. The sanctuary is called a meeting room.

It was all so new to me.

We walked down the corridor and took our seats. Little Colleen was excited about going to the children's session. At the beginning of the service, I noticed that the bishop was wearing a dark suit with a white shirt and black tie. He was clean-shaven, but had longish sideburns. He called the meeting to order and continued talking, making announcements about the various wards in town. I couldn't believe what I'd just heard.

Whoa, I thought, *wait a second*. Did he actually call what I thought was a Christian service a "meeting to order"?

The bishop was talking and gesturing to ten young men who wore black pants and white collared shirts. I noticed that they all looked and dressed alike. The young men started to pass around the bread and the little plastic cups with a pitcher of water. As modest and simple as the interior looked, which Liam had pointed out as a virtue, it was the very fact of how simple it was that took me aback. I was struck by the drab bareness of the room. There was nothing on the walls: no crosses, no crucifix, no statue of the Blessed Virgin Mary, no painting of the Prodigal Son, no altar with crisp white linens and gold goblets. There was only a podium with a microphone. There was no identifiable symbol or artwork to remind us that we were in a place dedicated to glorifying God. In the cold room, it felt like being at a company seminar, replete with the large pitchers of water and padded banquet chairs. As the bishop was talking about the young men and admiring their dedication, my ears started to ring; in a flash, the bishop resembled Jim Jones standing there with his white shirt, black tie, and syrupy smile. I felt my head slant so I could hear him better, and suddenly, out of nowhere, the word "cult" popped into my head so hard it felt like an explosion going off.

I wanted to jump up and run out of there as fast as I could. I looked around in each direction, left to right and back again. My heart was pounding. I pictured myself climbing over people, squeezing between them, stepping on their feet and then running out the back double doors into the foyer. At the same time, I felt a strong gravitational pull toward Liam. I even looked at him, then back at the bishop, and over to the jam-packed rows of people, wondering what was happening to me, and if I should stay there or run. And if I did run, where would I go?

I stayed seated and thought, *But I'm here with my husband.*

I put my hand out and reached over to Liam's; he held it gently with both of his hands. They were warm and reassuring. I felt my anxiety melt away.

After the first hour of what the Mormons called "the meeting," all the adults, men and women together, went into rooms in groups to read the Book of Mormon. I had never heard of this book, but I was told it had what the Bible was missing. Missing? Missing *what*, I wondered. Sherrie handed me a book, and people took turns reading out loud. Eventually Sherrie motioned for me to read, and she showed me where they were in the Book of Mormon. I looked at where she was pointing and silently read something about the Pearl of Great Price. My eyes couldn't focus on the page, and the words became blurry. I felt myself unable to talk. When I opened my mouth to speak, nothing came out. I vigorously shook my head, smiled, and mouthed the word "no." Everyone turned to look at me, but I was not going to read.

The third hour was spent in another meeting room, with the women and men separated. The women's-only meeting was called a Relief Society meeting, and the men's-only meeting was called a Priesthood meeting. In the women's group, they passed around a sign-up sheet for people to prepare dinner for the young men who were in the area for their mission. Sherrie told me how hard they worked, and that once a week she had them over to dinner at her house. I have always enjoyed cooking, and I certainly cooked every night for Liam and Hannah, but for some reason, the binder with the sign-up sheets felt like a hot potato. I couldn't get it out of my hands fast enough. Quickly, I slid the binder down the table to a lady sitting next to me. Before the meeting closed, I knew I could not go back to the Mormon church. In retrospect, I believe it was God's holy spirit telling me to get up and run out of there.

After lunch, I drove Sherrie and Dan to the airport, because Liam said the car was too crowded with all of us, and he had things to do. On the way back, I stopped at McDonald's for the grandkids. I was lost in thought driving when I decided that the best way to tell Liam that I couldn't go to his church anymore, nor could I continue in this situation, was to do it while the grandchildren were there. I was scared of what his reaction might be, and I knew he wouldn't do anything to harm me with the kids around. He was crazy about them, and was always striving to be the best grandpa; he wanted to prove that whatever their mother had told them about him, it was different now. I could tell that Liam wanted them to know he was an upright, respectable, and righteous man. I thought he was one, too.

A few days after Sherrie and Dan left for the Bahamas, when the grandkids were down for a nap, Liam walked into the kitchen after lunch. "When Hannah leaves for college, let's adopt a child," he said out of the blue.

"Adopt a child?" I slowly repeated.

"That's what a lot of families I grew up with did when the older kids had moved out," Liam said, as if it were no big deal.

Sitting at the kitchen table, I looked down at the checks I was writing for all the house bills—utilities, food, clothing, etc.—and wondered how in the world I would be able to afford and be responsible for *another* person. Just the thought of it was overwhelming.

"Liam," I said, my voice trailing off a bit, "I don't know how we could afford that."

Looking back, I guess you could say that that was the straw that broke the camel's back. The Mormon church really had me spooked, and then with Liam suggesting we adopt a child, I knew we needed to talk about things on a more serious level. The situation was coming to a head. Never mind that we hadn't been intimate for months.

At the beginning of our marriage, we'd engage in passionate, hours-long love fests that took place once or twice a week, but now we were down to twenty minutes, once or twice a *month*, and on Liam's terms. When I had brought up the fact that I missed our intimacy, and felt like I was in the desert, Liam replied with exasperation, "You got your dad to thank for that. He has me run ragged. I'm his whipping post, and I got nothin' left."

This was getting weird, I thought. I was not about to tell my dad to stop working Liam so hard, because he gets too tired to have sex with me. Nor could I see myself telling Liam to step up to the plate and man up, because I knew he thought he was already doing that, and so much more.

That evening, we put the grandkids to bed. Colleen slept in the big bed in the guest bedroom, and Danny slept in the Pack 'n Play. Liam and I each read the kids a story, then said bedtime prayers. I turned off the light, and when we walked out of the bedroom, I left the door ajar.

Feeling anxious, I started doing some laundry to calm my nerves. Liam had walked back into the office and taken up residence at the computer, as he'd been doing for the past couple of months. After dinner, we used to watch a movie or TV show together almost every night, but now Liam just went into the office and shut the glass panel French door.

Summoning my courage, I walked into the office. "We have to talk," I said.

We sat in the living room on the green suede sofas, in front of the big picture window. My mouth was dry, and my heart was pounding.

"I can't do this anymore," I stammered.

"What can't you do anymore?"

"Well," I started to say slowly, before it all came tumbling out. "I can't take the pressure of you and my dad arguing almost daily now. I can't take the pressure of being the sole provider for you and your family, and being the only one to bring in an income. Not only can I not do it financially, but my salary and the money I make from the farm can't continue to support all this at this rate. I also can't take the emotional pressure."

"Then you tell your dad you need more money to live on," Liam burst out. "You just tell him. You tell him you have to have more money, and he's not giving you enough for operating expenses for the household."

Liam wasn't hearing what I was saying.

"I can't do that," I said. "My dad has given me so much.

I'm not going to tell him to give me more money. It's not just the money. Can you please, *please* find another job? You said you had a great one before, I'm sure there are more out there. Didn't you say you knew the manager who worked in this region? Maybe he knows if there are any possible openings. Why don't you call him? I bet you could work in computers like you did before, plus it would bring in way more income, and you'd have more autonomy. That way, my dad wouldn't have to be your boss."

As I was talking, Liam kept shaking his head in short, back and forth motions, closing his eyes, then opening them.

"I've made huge sacrifices to be here and help you with this farm," Liam said. "Just like in Bob Dylan's song 'Maggie's Farm.'"

It always hurt when Liam brought up that song. The lyrics detail the indignities of working for Maggie's family, including her mean "pa."

Liam got up and went into the office, then came back in less than a minute. He started reading a love poem by Longfellow out loud, followed by part of what the commissioner had read when he married us.

"I vow," Liam started, "that this love will be my only true love…"

"Liam, please," I continued. "It's not that I don't love you. I love you so much, and you know that."

Liam kept reading and emphasizing the commitment we'd made to one another, as if I hadn't said anything.

"Liam, please," I pleaded again. "We know a lot about the farm now. I've been recording things for the last ten years, and the whole time you and I have been married. We're okay. If something happens to my dad, I have all that we need to keep the farm going, or at least to the best of our abilities."

Liam was adamant about not getting another job. "I've told you, I gave up a huge career to be here, and that's gone now, that's in the past. I'm here, and I'm going to keep doing what I'm doing, just like we planned."

By that point, I felt like I was up against a brick wall, and there was no way to break through it. I did not want another divorce. Yet I didn't know what else to do.

"I can't do this anymore," I told Liam. "If you can't get another job, then I don't think I can go on in this relationship."

"What do you mean?" Liam asked abruptly. All of a sudden, his entire demeanor changed from lovey-dovey to hardline.

"I don't think I can continue in this relationship," I repeated.

Liam kept pressing. "What does that mean?"

"I don't want a divorce," I said. "I really don't. I don't know what to do if you don't get another job. I think this is what has been causing my migraines."

"Oh, you're going to blame your headaches on the marriage?" Liam said, trivializing my health.

So many thoughts raced through my mind. Liam's religious faith was one of the things that had drawn me to him in the first place. He presented himself as a pinnacle of virtue; he could even quote scripture. He had this reverent, righteous "Man of God" persona, and yet, things just weren't matching up. The Mormon Church had been troubling me, too. I didn't like the fact that nonmembers—people who were not Mormon— were forbidden from entering their temples during a marriage ceremony. The God I believed in was not discriminatory when it came to who could enter a place of worship and adoration. If a Mormon is from out of town, they need to have a written recommendation from the bishop of their ward to allow them to enter, and if a parent or sibling is not Mormon, they cannot be a part of the wedding ceremony.

"Maybe you want to be with someone who is Mormon," I said. And, for the first time, I said clearly, "I'm not going to become Mormon."

"I never asked you to become Mormon," Liam snapped. "No one ever said anything about that."

"Why then did you have all your records from the ward in Tucson sent here, and why are you wearing those white things under your clothes now every day, and why did those missionary people come here to the house a couple of times last week? You told me it was to get me to become Mormon, because they knew I wasn't."

"No one said you had to become Mormon," Liam repeated.

"Oh, really?" I said. "Yeah, right, how is that going to work? You going to the Mormon church every weekend for hours, and volunteering there, like you said, during the week in the evenings. What am I going to do then, cook dinner for the missionaries who show up here on their bicycles every night?"

Liam was really starting to get mad now, although I could tell he was keeping his temper in check. Because of the grandkids, we had to talk softly. "How dare you bring this up now, when the grandkids are here?" Liam said.

Exactly, I thought. Thank goodness they're here. Those sleeping, sweet little munchkins had saved me incalculable amounts of trauma, I was sure of it.

As Liam got up from the sofa, he said, "I feel sick. You're asking me for a divorce. I can't talk anymore right now."

"Liam," I said. "I'm not asking you for a divorce, I'm asking you to get another job. But you keep refusing to do that. I'm up against a wall. I'm getting complete resistance from you. I tell you that I love you, and yet, I don't really feel that you love me the same way I love you. That it's not me you love, but what I have."

As he stalked out of the living room and headed into the office, Liam said, "I need to process this."

The next morning, before the grandkids were up, Liam threw open the double doors to our bedroom and said loudly, "Well, are we going to get a divorce or not?"

It took me aback. I was sound asleep, and looking at him standing there, still wearing his clothes from the previous day, I realized that he had never come to bed during the night. I had been so exhausted, and had experienced such a huge emotional meltdown that I'd fallen dead asleep for the whole night.

"I don't want a divorce," I reiterated, as I sat up in bed.

I couldn't imagine life without Liam, yet I didn't know how to continue. All I knew was that I could no longer live with the situation the way it was.

Liam and I had promised the grandkids we would take them swimming at my parents' house that afternoon. Right before we were about to leave, Liam said he had some things to do at the house, what, I didn't know, so I took the kids by myself. On the way, I stopped and bought them popsicles. At the pool, I lathered each one of them up with sunscreen, put floaties on Danny's arms, and made sure that Colleen stayed in the shallow end. Holding Danny, I taught him how to kick in the water, and played with him on the steps.

When the grandkids and I got back, Liam told me that he had called Sherrie in the Bahamas. He'd told her that we had some issues to take care of, and that they would need to arrange a flight out right away and come pick up the kids. Originally, they had planned to stay another week with us after they returned from the Bahamas.

When Saturday came, I did not want to go pick up Dan

and Sherrie at the airport. Their flight arrived at 9:00 p.m. in San Francisco, and their morning flight was at 8:00 a.m. out of Oakland. It was late getting back, and early to start in the morning, especially for their children. I suggested that Liam pick up Dan and Sherrie while I stayed with the kids, but he was insistent that we all go to the airport together. My SUV held seven passengers, although it was a tight fit with barely enough room for the luggage. After we put the kids in the car seats, Liam told me to get in, and that he was driving. The hour-and-forty-five-minute drive to the airport was strained and uncomfortable. Liam hardly spoke to me.

After we picked up Dan and Sherrie, he got into the passenger side seat and said, "You drive." I tried to talk while I was driving, but when I asked a question Liam didn't allow time for Sherrie to answer. He talked right over me, as if I wasn't there, and as though Sherrie couldn't have heard my voice.

The next morning, when it was time to load up the car and take them all to the Oakland airport, which was closer than SFO, I said to Liam, "I'm going to stay home. That way there will be more room, and you all can visit."

Liam looked at me and said, "No, you are going."

"No, no, it's okay," I said. "You all go, there's hardly enough room as it is. I don't mind staying home."

Liam put his hand on my elbow, gave it a slight push toward the car door, and said in a matter-of-fact way, "You are going."

I know I had a puzzled look on my face, because Sherrie and Dan and the kids looked at me, as if there were no question about whether or not I was going. They kept smiling at me. In hindsight, they resembled the friendly, strangely beautiful Cullen family in the movie *Twilight*. I felt awkward, trapped between the family "outing" to the airport and the altercation I'd had with Liam. It felt like I had no choice, though, so I

went, and the car was even more crowded this time. Because
of the kids' suitcases, which Dan had put on his lap, along
with the bags around his feet on the floor, I could hardly move.

Later that same day, back from the airport, Liam said to me
without any emotion, "I'm going to Tucson to get my résumé.
I've been thinking, since we already have a lot of knowledge
about the farm, I can look for something else to do."

I couldn't believe my ears. Yes, those were my words that
he'd repeated verbatim, but it didn't matter to me if he wanted
to make them his. It was such a relief to hear him tell me that
he was going to look for another job.

Except, *Whoa, wait a minute,* I thought.

"Why can't you work on it here?" I asked Liam. "You're
going to go all the way to Tucson just to get your résumé?"

"Yep," he said shortly. "I'm going to go get my résumé and
get it up to date," he continued, vehemently nodding his head,
"and finish the studio, so I can rent it out to get some income
from it."

I had this dreadful feeling that if Liam left, he wouldn't come
back for a long time. There would be no incentive for him to
return. For some reason, I could see him stringing it out and
hanging out in Tucson for six months. It was too open-ended,
and I was afraid he would just keep asking me to send him
money.

Once again, I did not like this situation, but I didn't know
how to change it.

"Oh," he continued, "I'll need a couple thousand bucks for
repairs on the studio. Oh, and a little spending money for
groceries and living."

I felt my heart squeeze. His requests for money made me
sad, and yet at the same time I had an intense fear that he
wouldn't come back. As much as he upset me, I could still feel

the magnetic pull.

"Liam," I said. "Please don't go. You have all the information you need to work on your résumé here. It's on your computer."

"No," he said, shaking his head back and forth with those familiar short motions. "I've got the quad runner ready to load on the truck. I'm taking it down to the Honda store to see how much I can get for it. I'll probably get a couple of thousand from that, but I'll still need a few thousand more from you."

"But wait, I bought that for the farm," I said. "It's licensed and insured here, and you know it's got those special wires for the boom sprayer and the small trailer."

I had paid $8,000 for the four-wheel quad for the fields, which Liam had insisted I buy so he could ride around and check the trees. I didn't want to have to replace it with a new one.

Liam continued with his reasoning. "The faster I get the studio rented, the faster I'll get back to find a job. I've got quite a few repairs, and I need money to get the place ready. Larry's waiting for me down at the Honda store. I've got to go."

"Okay," I said. "I'll give you the money."

He said he needed $5,000, so I wrote him a check. I was up against a wall. Buying a new quad runner would cost the same amount, so what was the difference, I figured. Besides, if I bought a new one, how would I explain that to Arturo?

After I handed Liam the check, he went out to put the quad back in the garage. Then he started packing up his office things, and for the next couple of days, he tidied up in the garage and packed some clothes. Whenever we had an errand to run, he would make a big, drawn-out, dramatic point for us to leave together. He would also wait until I set the alarm before he left the house.

One day in particular, he said that he was going to give blood and do a couple of errands in town. I did not take note of it at the time, nor did I wonder why, but in hindsight, I realized that Liam had stood there waiting by the door, making a point that I would not be in the house by myself. I went over to my parents' ranch, as usual, but I happened to come back a little early that day, and I arrived before Liam did. I was standing in the office by his computer, and had the doors open to a large credenza next to his briefcase.

When Liam walked in, he immediately said in a rapid staccato, "HEY, HEY, HEY. What are you doing in here?"

"I'm getting out some printer paper," I replied. "I need it for the ranch office."

"You're back already? You said you weren't going to be back till noon."

At that point, I noticed Liam lift his foot and use it to slide his briefcase over the hardwood floor to a corner by the big credenza. That motion stood out in my mind.

When he went out to the garage for a few minutes, I tried to see what was in his briefcase. I was curious about what was in there that he didn't want me to see, but the briefcase was so jam-packed with papers that I couldn't even pry them apart to read at an angle. The briefcase was literally bulging at the seams. *Oh, well,* I thought, *whatever.*

The next day we went over to my dad's house. It was Liam's idea to tell him that he was going to Tucson to work on some things there. In the kitchen, as Liam started to give my dad the news, I went into my office and quickly typed up a resignation letter for Liam to sign. The letter stated that he would be unable to work for a while, and that he was resigning and didn't know when he would return. I had been paying him for the last four weeks, even though my dad didn't want me to, and I was now at the point that if Liam wasn't going to be there, and was no longer working for my dad, and was going to get his résumé in a different state so that he could look for another job, it ought to be in writing. My accountant had told me to put it in writing whenever an employee quit voluntarily, and Liam was an employee doing just that.

When I brought the letter back into the kitchen, Liam and my dad were sitting across from one another at the table. I made sure to explain that our accountant requested this form from people who quit voluntarily. I could tell that Liam did not want to sign the resignation letter. He started to hesitate, looked at me, then over at the live-in caregiver who helped my dad and Charlotte, and finally at my dad.

"I'll sign it after you," my dad said.

Liam looked down at the letter, then back at my dad.

"You sign it first," he said, and gently pushed the paper across the table.

It looked like a duel in slow motion as they took turns pushing the letter back and forth across the wooden table a few times, insisting that the other one sign first. Finally, my dad capitulated and signed it first. I made a copy of the letter, gave it to Liam, and kept the original in the ranch office.

The next morning, Liam woke up at 5:00 a.m. He stepped into the bathroom to take a shower, but strangely, he left the door wide open. At the same time, I glanced over and saw his briefcase by the closet door. There it was again. I wondered if Liam had left the bathroom door open so he could see if I got out of bed and looked in the briefcase. It was so packed that I figured he had the computer I'd bought him, along with whatever else, stuffed inside.

As I watched him get dressed and throw some more clothes into the suitcases, I had misgivings about his departure. He kissed me goodbye and said, "I love you. I'll be back soon. Just as soon as I get my résumé together and the studio fixed up."

As he spoke, he looked over his shoulder at his briefcase, then back at me. He had this smirk on his face, and even though he said, "I love you," for the last time, he also flashed a simpering half-smile and nodded his head up and down.

A couple of hours later, he called me from the road. He said he was going through Fresno and might lose cell connection; he wanted me to know in case I tried calling him. He called quite a few times throughout the day, and when he got to Tucson, he called again to let me know that he'd arrived safely.

At first, we talked on the phone a couple of times a day. One morning, when Liam was talking about the house, he said "we." When I asked him who "we" was, he told me it was the person helping him with the studio. This struck me as odd.

It had been about five days since he'd left, and I was at my house. I grabbed my treasured Almond Timeline from the office shelf. Liam had a fancy name for it. He called it the Production Manual for Succession Planning. As I lifted the normally very heavy binder to put some documents inside, I immediately noticed that it almost hit the shelf above because it was so much lighter than usual. Its weightlessness scared me, and my heart started to pound.

I ran into the kitchen and opened it up on the table. All that was left were the month dividers, January through December, and a few notes stuffed into the pocket of the inside cover. All of my papers had been three-hole punched, and somebody would have to have pulled pretty hard to get the two-inch, three-ring binder to pop open. All of the handwritten notes that I'd made with my dad over the past ten years were gone. The typed documents were gone. The information that my dad had shared with me over days and months and years, including the production numbers for each field, each variety of nut, and each year, were all gone. I had written about problems that came up and how we'd fixed them. I had written short stories and recorded anecdotes that my dad had told me about his family and four generations of farming.

Who would take those papers? Why?

Liam, I thought. He was the only one who knew where I kept the binder.

I called him immediately. "My papers are gone," I said, as soon as he picked up the phone. "Do you know where they are?"

"What papers?" he said.

"My papers out of my Almond Timeline." I could hear my voice quivering. "They're all gone. Did you take them?"

"No," he said. "They're around there somewhere."

We went back and forth in a verbal volley. I'd ask him why he took them, and then he'd deny it. He told me I was losing things all the time, and this was one of those things again. That wasn't true. The only time I couldn't find an important file within five minutes was when I had to procure Hannah's driver's license information for her permit appointment. It turned out to be in the file right where I thought it was; it had just been put back behind a bigger manila folder, and so it was hard to see. Now Liam was using this against me to say that I lost things all the time.

I called him back an hour later and asked again, "Where are my papers?" By then, I was beside myself. I had spent years recording the information that was in that binder. Once again, he denied having taken my papers. "Yeah, right," I said, "and am I supposed to believe that the cat ate them?"

"As soon as I get back, I'll help you find them," he said.

Help me find them? That was crazy.

"Oh, and what are you going to do?" I said. "Plant them when you get back to make me think they were here all along?"

A few more days passed, and I called Liam again to ask him

to please mail my papers back. He just kept saying that he didn't take them.

"When I get back there," he said, "we're going to go see a marriage counselor."

"That's a great idea," I said.

"Marriage is built on trust."

"Yes," I said emphatically. "That's right."

"There's something wrong with you that you don't trust me. You're paranoid, and we're going to go see a doctor when I get back."

"Well, that's not going to work, and you know it," I said. "You sitting there, lying to a marriage counselor, denying that you took my papers. How is that going to work?"

"We're going to the doctor, that's how it's going to work."

"This is going nowhere," I said, and hung up shortly after.

I went out into the backyard and looked up at the redwood trees, wondering what I was going to do. The whole conversation scared me to death. Since Liam had taken my papers and lied about it, what would he, or could he, lie about next?

Two days later, Liam called at 6:00 a.m. In an unexpected turn of events, he told me that his foster father, Henry, had just died. A couple of years earlier, Henry had come to visit us, and we had taken him on a ride around the fields. He was a pleasant, good-natured man.

"Considering what you and I have going on right now," Liam said, hesitating and stammering a bit. "I'm going to need you to send me my suit."

I fell quiet. Here I had been begging him to send me my papers back, and all of a sudden, he was asking me to send him his suit.

Going with my first instinct, I said, "I'll send you your suit." It was the one I had bought him for my mom's funeral.

"You will?" he asked.

"Liam," I said. "When have I ever said no to you for anything?"

Later, though, I couldn't stop thinking about it. I did not want to send him his suit, yet I felt I had to, given that it was for a funeral. It was my natural sympathetic response. I called Dr. Paxton, the psychiatrist I had been seeing before Liam and I got married, to ask him what I should do. "Don't send him the suit until he sends you your papers," said Dr. Paxton.

I took the advice and called Liam back a few hours later.

"I'm not going to send you your suit until you send me my papers back," I said, asserting my authority with him for the first time ever.

Had it not been for Dr. Paxton giving me what I felt like was permission to say this, permission to say *something* that I knew the other person wouldn't like, I don't think I would have had the courage. It was in direct contradiction to my people-pleasing psyche. Liam hung up on me, but he called back about an hour later and screamed, "You take my suit down to FedEx, and you send it to me *today*, and then you email me the tracking number. How dare you not send me my suit after all that I have done for you. I helped you when your mom died. You send me my suit today. Do you hear me?"

I had never heard Liam scream or hyperventilate like that. He was so mad, and talking so loudly and aggressively that I could hear the spit coming out of his mouth as he yelled over the phone.

"No, I'm not sending it to you," I yelled back. My own adrenaline was starting to pump. "I'm the one who should be telling *you* to send those papers back to *me* and, oh, by the way, email me the FedEx tracking number, you got that?"

"You're waterboarding me," he roared. "You're harassing me.

I don't have them. This is abusive."

When he said the word "have," his voice sounded high-pitched.

"Then who *does have* them, Liam? Who did you give those papers to?"

I felt like I was on to something.

"I'm tired of you harassing me," he fumed, and hung up the phone.

The next day I brought home a huge box from FedEx. I packed up his dress shoes, belt, socks, casual pants, and some collared shirts. I also included some memoirs Henry had written, in case Liam wanted to refer to them at the funeral home.

When I took the box to FedEx to mail it, I put in a prepaid, self-addressed envelope so that Liam could put my papers in it and send them back to me.

The day after the box arrived, Liam called. "I got the box with my suit," was all he said.

"Oh, good," I said, "then that means you got the FedEx envelope. All you have to do is put my papers in it and drop it off."

It was quiet on the other end of the phone. "Are you there?" I asked.

Liam completely ignored what I had just said and closed with, "Wanted you to know I got the box. See ya."

I was considering going to Illinois for Henry's funeral, because as angry as I was with Liam, I still wanted to see him. I knew he was lying when he said he didn't have my papers, but at the same time, I wanted to be there for him. I couldn't reconcile these opposing feelings within myself. I knew that if I saw Liam again, we would probably get back together, and by this time, I knew that would not be good for me.

I was beginning to realize that Liam was both toxic and magnetic. Like someone addicted to a substance, I was both physically and mentally dependent on him. Liam was my substance.

17

Funnel Cloud

I waited a week, hoping that Liam might actually reciprocate, but I never got that FedEx envelope. In the meantime, we spoke on the phone a couple of times. On a Sunday, he told me that he was flying to Illinois for the funeral that coming Thursday. He also said he didn't know the name of the hotel where he was staying, which I thought was strange. When I spoke to him again on Tuesday, he told me that he was leaving the next day.

"Oh, you changed your flight?" I said, surprised.

"No, I didn't," he said. "You've got that mixed up."

I knew I didn't have it mixed up. I had been asking Liam about his travel arrangements because the part of me that still wanted to be with him was winning out. I wanted to join him in Illinois, but now it was impossible; his sudden change in plans had left me no time to make my own arrangements. It seemed as if Liam had mixed up the days on purpose so that I wouldn't be able to attend Henry's funeral.

By the end of the week, I knew that Liam had flown to Illinois for Henry's funeral, and I still had not received my papers. I didn't know what to do. I didn't want a divorce, but I didn't want to be driven into financial ruin, either. I started to wonder if I could even afford to divorce Liam. What would he be entitled to? How much would it cost? Would I have to pay for my legal fees *and* his legal fees? It was painful to think about. How could I divorce someone who I was so in love with?

I thought to call the attorney whom I'd used for my divorce with Dale and ask her these questions. Upon filling her in, she gave me the name of a highly acclaimed attorney in my county, since it would be in my best interest to have someone local. I called the lawyer right away and made an appointment.

The next day, I drove to the attorney's office and sat outside in the car, debating whether or not to go in, wishing I hadn't made the appointment in the first place. A few minutes later, I thought, *Okay, since I did make the appointment, I should go in to be respectful and at the very least say, "Thank you, but everything is fine. I'm sorry for wasting your time."*

It didn't go that way. After I gave the lawyer, Meghan Evans, a recap of the past seven years, which took a while, she in turn told me things about Liam in ten minutes that had taken me seven years to figure out. Meghan was wise beyond her years. She was an astute woman with broad knowledge of the law and a clear understanding of human psychology. She linked the evidence for me that day, convincing me that I was not dealing with a normal person. Her advice was to make use of the opportunity right away. "Strike while the iron is hot," she said. She explained that because Liam had been living in my house for the past five years, he was entitled to half of its ownership. I was shocked; my previous attorney had not mentioned anything about cohabitation in a home that I owned. I'd assumed that it was considered separate property, just like my dad's cousin had told me. But Meghan said that even though I had bought the house before we were married, since it had also been Liam's residence, by law it was his house, too.

"You're lucky you've only been married for five years," she said.

"What do you mean?" I asked.

"Well," she said, "in California, if the divorce takes place after ten years of marriage, then the court has jurisdiction to determine that the financially supportive spouse pay alimony for life. He probably knows that," she said.

This meant that if the marriage lasted ten years, I would be paying Liam alimony for the rest of my life. I wanted to follow Meghan's advice and act fast, but my heart and emotions held me back. My therapist, Dr. Rose, had also been telling me to act fast. She'd even used the same words as Meghan: "Strike while the iron is hot."

Dr. Rose was a forensic clinical psychologist from England, with a quick wit and a British accent. She was also Catholic, and had spent many years studying theology. I'd first worked with her during my divorce with Dale, and went on to see her during my courtship with Liam. She had been the one to refer me to Dr. Paxton. Before I consulted with Meghan, I called Dr. Rose because she told it like it was, and I trusted her opinion. She could not have been more direct. "Act fast; you need to divorce him right now," she'd said. Her words sounded harsh and radical, and I didn't want to hear them. I did not want to divorce Liam.

Meghan told me that if I was going to file for divorce, I had to file immediately, and have Liam served with the divorce papers in Tucson. If I didn't, and I filed when he came back, the law provided that he could take half of my house. "How do you know that he isn't going to file against you?" Meghan asked.

"Oh, he wouldn't do that," I said.

I could hardly imagine my own self doing this. Divorcing the love of my life, the person who every winter night warmed my side of the bed while he waited up for me, so that when I got in he could hold me tight and whisper "I love you" in my ear. *How could I go through with this?* I thought. When I talked to Liam, I felt deceitful, as if I were the bad person, because I didn't want to mention what was I considering doing.

I thought about it night and day. I thought about how he kept saying that he knew nothing about my papers, until he said he didn't *have* them. I knew right then, as soon as Liam said that, that either he did have them, or he'd given them to someone else. I'm not a detective, but in my mind, if you say you don't "have" something, it implies that you did have it at one time. Maybe Liam really was going to file for divorce, as Meghan had suggested.

The day after Liam returned from the funeral, I called him and gave him one more chance to tell me that he'd taken the papers from my Almond Timeline. If he would only be honest, I thought, then I would forget the whole thing. I told him that if he didn't tell me the truth, I was going to have to do something about this situation. I could no longer live like this. Our conversation went in circles, and it was clear that he was not going to admit what he'd done, or return my papers.

That afternoon, I called Meghan, drove to her office, and signed the documents to initiate the process of divorcing Liam. When I got back to my house, I curled up on my bed in the fetal position and cried and cried. I felt sick to my stomach, and I was shaking and freezing cold. I kept rocking myself back and forth.

Right then, my dad happened to knock on the door. *What timing,* I thought. I didn't want to talk to him about it, or have him know anything until the whole thing was over. But since my car was parked in the driveway, and my dad knew I was home, I had to answer the door and pretend like everything was okay. I splashed water on my face and quickly brushed my hair.

I opened the door and said, "Hi, Dad."

"Hi," he said. "Just stopped by to visit."

"That's nice," I said. "But I'm not feeling well. I was about to go lie down."

"Oh, okay," he said. "Hope you feel better. I'll talk to you tomorrow."

After my dad left, I went back to my bedroom, fell on my bed, and stayed there for the rest of the evening.

The following week, a process server went to Liam's house and served him with the divorce papers. Later that day, while I was showing the house that he'd insisted we buy in order to flip— but he'd never actually fixed up—Liam called. I looked at my caller ID, then at the potential tenant. "Can you give me a second?" I said. "I need to answer this."

"Hello?" I said.

"I was just delivered something," Liam snarled. "You're going to be sorry for this, I can tell you that right now. You have just made a very bad mistake," he said, and hung up the phone.

Half an hour later, as I was showing the house to another prospective tenant, Liam's best friend's girlfriend called me. She was aghast at what was happening. The first thing she said was, "Don't tell Liam that I called you. Don't tell anyone, I can't talk long. Barry might break up with me if he knows that I called you, but I just had to tell you that Liam and Barry are talking about taking everything you own."

I couldn't speak. Liam's best friend was a family law attorney and had represented him in his previous divorces.

"I told them they can't do that," she went on to say. "Liam is so mad, and they said that they are going to try to do whatever they can to take everything he can get from you. Are you there?" she asked.

"Yes," I answered. I was in shock. The prospective renter was standing there, looking at me. I motioned with my hand to wait.

"I gotta go," Barry's girlfriend said. "Don't tell them, or anyone, I called you."

"Okay," I said, and we both hung up.

I was shaken. It was 5:30 p.m., and I knew that Meghan had left her office for the day. I would have to wait until the next day to speak with her.

At 6:00 a.m. the next morning, I called Melinda, my running partner from college. We were both early birds, and I knew she would be awake. When I told her what was going on, she said, "I'm not surprised. There was something about Liam that didn't seem right. I bet he's been planning this all along."

"You really think so?" I said. "It's so hard for me to believe."

"Well, yes," she said. "Now we know his true motives."

A couple of hours later, I called Meghan, who told me not to worry. "Let's wait to see his response to our initial filing," she said.

"Okay," I said, but I was still worried about Liam's intentions.

Ten days later, Meghan called to tell me that she had received Liam's response, and he had agreed to appear in court. The substance of his response only confirmed my worst fears. According to what Liam and his lawyer had written, since he, Liam, had bettered my separate property for the length of our marriage, he was entitled to complete compensation. The response went on to say that Liam would prove his qualitative and quantitative betterment of my property by providing documentation to a forensic accountant.

Based on this response, it was glaringly apparent that Liam had taken the contents of my Almond Timeline so as to use the information in it to demonstrate his supposed knowledge of the farm, and to claim that he had been the primary decision maker. In reality, it was *my* knowledge of the farm, not his. If he knew so much about the farm, why would he need to take my Almond Timeline?

"*That* is why he took my papers," I told Meghan.

Could it really be, I asked myself, *that Liam had been planning this all along?* All of his talk about succession planning, and chronicling the farm's operations in my Almond Timeline so the kids would know how to run it in the future, was probably for his benefit. He wanted my Almond Timeline so that he could take credit for all of the work my family had performed, and I had so diligently recorded.

"If Liam were to hire a forensic accountant," I said to Meghan. "They would see that the original papers were mine."

"I know exactly how to prove that," she said. "We'll hire a handwriting analyst to show that the originals were in your handwriting, not Liam's. That would prove that he stole your farm's intellectual property."

"That would be great," I said, "but I doubt that he would use my originals. They were written in longhand, and he probably had his lawyer's secretary decipher them and type all of the information into her computer. I have a feeling that when Liam left for Tucson, he dropped my papers off at his attorney's main law office in Fresno."

"He most likely knew that by giving your papers to his attorney, they became protected under attorney-client privilege," Meghan said.

"I'm almost positive that's what he did," I said, "because I recently looked up the cell phone records for that day. They placed him right there in Fresno, along with a phone number to that very law office. Who would know that the originals were mine? No one except for me and Liam, and that is why he could not and would not tell me the truth. The truth was not in his plan."

18

Wedge Tornado

When the first divorce hearing came, I felt a sense of melancholy. Divorce court was the last place I ever imagined I'd find myself in again. During my first divorce, I'd had to go to court twice to fight over custody of my kids. The morning of the hearing with Liam, I thought to myself, *How hard could this one be without children involved?*

I had planned to meet my attorney at her office, then walk over to the courthouse in Patterson, the same one where Liam and I had been married five years earlier. Before I left the house, however, Meghan's assistant called and said, "Another lawyer in the office will be taking Meghan's place today in court."

"Oh, no," I replied.

"Meghan has a sick child home from school," she continued. "So she won't be in today."

"Okay," I said.

What could I do? Here I had spent hours with Meghan

discussing my case, and now I'd be represented by somebody I'd never met. Then the phone rang again; this time it was the actual attorney, a Mr. Scalise, whom I'd be meeting. He asked if I owed any money on the house that I shared with Liam. I told him that I'd bought it before I sold my other residence, so my parents had loaned me half the money. He wanted to know if I had something showing the amount I'd purchased it for, or any form of documentation showing the loan amount I still owed to my parents. The loan note was in my office at my dad's, and I had no time to retrieve it.

I had planned on wearing my wedding ring. I wanted Liam to see it on my finger and know that I still loved him. I knew he was lying to me, yet while half of me believed that he was lying, the other half of me was desperately ignoring this truth. I felt like I was having an internal fight with myself. My brain and my heart were clashing.

Feeling rattled, I was barely going to make it to the court-house on time. I raced out the door, jumped in the car, and was halfway to the law office when I realized that I had forgotten my wedding ring. If I went back to get it, I knew that it would take fifteen minutes and I would be late for the hearing. I hesitated. I didn't want to take the risk, but I really wanted to wear that ring. Since I didn't know where we were in the lineup at the courthouse, I decided to go on ahead without my wedding ring.

When I got to downtown Patterson, I parked in the garage a half a mile away from my attorney's office and ran to meet him. As we were walking to the courthouse, he asked me a few questions in preparation, which I was glad for at the time, because it helped to distract me from my nervousness.

"Were there any emails where Liam said when he would be back from Tucson?"

"No," I answered.

"He never said when he would be coming back?"

"No," I said again, this time with emphasis.

Mr. Scalise asked me again, "Are you sure? No emails with a date, or any indication of when he would be back?"

"No," I answered again, this time shaking my head. "Not one email at all. We've only talked on the phone, and not that much. I gave him five thousand dollars because he said if I didn't, he was going to sell a utility vehicle that we used on the farm, and he left without a word about when he would be coming back. Whenever I've asked him, he's left it completely open-ended. 'However long it takes, baby,' he always says."

Even though I was matter-of-factly telling all this to my attorney, inside I still felt a deep longing for Liam. It made no sense.

When I saw Liam in the crowded courtroom, my heart jumped. I had not seen him for six weeks. We did not speak. Mr. Scalise and I sat down at the table next to his, facing the judge. I noticed as Liam was sitting there that he was flaunting his own wedding ring, spinning it around and around on his finger. I was flabbergasted. I watched him make a great show of this, displaying the ring by placing his left hand at an angle on the table, and pointing it down in an obvious manner toward me and the female judge. This blatant exhibition made me feel sad that I wasn't wearing mine, but at the same time, I thought Liam looked kind of pretentious. I wanted to wear my ring because I still loved him, but was he wearing his for me, or for the judge?

After a lot of legal jargon, the lawyers and the judge, Barbara Holland, did all of the talking pertinent to our case. Liam's attorney told Judge Holland that his client, Mr. O'Connor, had nowhere to go, and since he had rented out his house in

Tucson, could he be granted access back into the home that he shared with me, Ms. Bennett?

I wrote a note to my attorney and slid it over to him. "Ask the judge to request a copy of the rental agreement," I wrote, "because I know that Liam is lying. He has not rented out his house, and he is living there right now."

Liam was given a week to show the court proof that he had rented out his home.

At the end of the hearing, the judge granted Liam access to come back and live at my house, and I was ordered to allow him to do so.

"Maybe he's had a change of heart," the judge said, looking directly at me.

When the lawyers approached the bench, I overheard the judge say something to Liam's attorney about the case. "And you'll represent him up here…the case will be brought up here…" I logged those comments away in my head, because they confirmed my suspicion that Liam had indeed dropped my papers off in Fresno the same day he'd left for Arizona. His lawyer's firm was headquartered in Fresno, which was south of Patterson, and so for the judge to say "you'll represent him up here" implied that Liam had originally consulted with lawyers down there.

Of course, I thought, *because that's where he'd dropped off my papers.*

I went into the hall to call Hannah and LeeAnn and let them know that Liam would be moving back into the house. In my heart I was excited about him coming back, and I was glad that it was the court that had ordered it, not me. I wasn't sure how it was going to work, but all I knew was that I desperately wanted to see Liam.

After I walked back to the office with my attorney, I got in my car and made a quick stop at my dad's to check on things there. I knew that Liam was going back to his attorney's office, because I'd overheard them talking about that, too.

When I got home, I was surprised Liam wasn't there. Timing-wise, he should have arrived at the house before me. When I walked into the house, LeeAnn said she had seen him pull into the driveway and up to the garage. He'd sat there for a few minutes, she told me, and then left.

He had called and left a message on my cell phone, but it was still on silent mode from the hearing. I listened to his message. "Hey, honey. Going to grab a sandwich, and then I'll be on the way over. Love you." Liam's voice was eerily calm, almost scripted. He called me "honey" and said "love you"? We had just been in court, where I had tried to block him from moving back in, and now he was talking to me as if nothing had happened? Like we had just been at the park or something. At the time, I did not allow myself to acknowledge how strange Liam's behavior was.

As usual, I knew better, but I buried it. I was dying to see him.

I went out to the garage and waited. A few minutes passed. Liam slowly pulled up into the gravel driveway in the Ford pickup. I started to rush out to see him, but stopped when I realized I had my glasses on. It wasn't that long ago that Liam had told me in no uncertain terms that he did not like my glasses. He said they were always smudged, and wondered how I could see through them. I told him I didn't mind. "Well, I mind," he'd retorted. "Why don't you get some contacts." That comment really stung, so when he drove up, I took off my glasses in the garage and set them on a shelf by the back door.

I ran up to him as he was getting out of the pickup. He smiled and said he had been there earlier, but he couldn't get in because his garage door opener didn't work. *Oh my gosh, that's right,* I thought. I'd had the code changed so that if Liam came back from Tucson late at night and I was asleep, he couldn't surprise me. He'd have to call me on the cell phone.

Liam walked briskly by me, still smiling and talking in that same eerily calm and monotone voice. As he walked into the house, I grabbed another garage door opener with the new code. I thought, *I better get this into his pickup, so he can't tell his attorney or the judge that I didn't allow him back in the house.* I had the new garage door opener in my hand. I opened up the passenger side door and stepped up into the pickup. I sat on the passenger side seat and tried to reach over with my left hand to take the old one down off the driver's side visor. This was not a big truck. It was a Ford F-150 single cab with a tiny seat in the middle that the console went down over. There wasn't a large expanse between the driver's side and the passenger's side. I had made this reach numerous times before, because the remote was on the righthand side of the driver's visor. This was the same pickup truck that I'd bought from my dad for Liam, so I was very familiar with it.

Again, I tried to reach over to take the old remote down, and this time I twisted around using my right hand, but again, it was so weird: I couldn't reach it. It was right in front of me, and yet for some reason, I couldn't reach it, as if something invisible was in my way. All of a sudden, I felt pressure pushing up against the back of my bottom and thigh. I looked down and thought, *What is this? What am I sitting on?* It was a big, fat manila folder. I pulled the folder out from underneath me and opened it. I had the pile of papers face down, and with my right hand, I tried to skim through it like a deck of cards, but since I didn't have my glasses on, I couldn't make out the words.

"HEY, HEY, HEY. What are you doing?" Liam yelled.

He was running toward me out of the garage. With each

"hey," his voice got louder and louder, in rapid staccato, until he was standing right next to me; in a flash he ripped the whole stack of papers, with the manila folder and all, right out of my hands. It was the same rapid staccato from the time he'd found me in the office, standing by the credenza near his brief-case, when he'd discreetly tried to slide it away with his foot.

"What are you doing?" he snapped. He grabbed my arm and said, "Get out of my truck NOW. Get out."

I scrambled off the seat onto the driveway and stammered, "I was trying to put a new remote in your pickup, since the one you have doesn't work anymore."

"Stay out of there," he said, as he yanked the remote out of my other hand and walked around to the driver's side. He got into the pickup and backed out with tires spinning and gravel flying, then turned it around so that the back was up against the garage, and the passenger side door was blocked by redwood trees and the fence. Then he locked the truck.

"What are all those papers?" I asked.

He paused and said, "Those are the documents from the court filings."

"You know and I know that there were only a few pages that each of us filed," I said.

I realized then that they had to be copies of my original papers from the Almond Timeline. But how was I going to get them now that he had the pickup truck turned around, locked, and parked up against the trees?

I followed Liam back into the house. He went straight into the bedroom closet, where he started pulling out drawers, emptying his shorts and socks into black plastic garbage bags. Next, he took tall stacks of his T-shirts that I had folded extra neatly and shoved those in the bags, too. I had learned how to do a traditional dress shirt fold when I'd worked as a manager at Bloomingdale's. Whether it was a T-shirt or pajamas, I folded everything that way. All of Liam's clothes that I had kept so tidily for him after doing his laundry were now just a mishmash of stuff, like they had been tossed in a blender.

"What are you doing?" I said, looking at him. "I thought you were moving back in?"

"I think it's best I don't," he said.

"But you told the judge you had nowhere to go. What are you doing? Where are you going to go?"

"I'm going to go stay with friends," he said matter-of-factly.

That seemed scripted, too. The only friends I knew that he could stay with were Greg and Susie, who lived in Lake Havasu, on the way back to Tucson. The fact that Liam didn't tell me who he was going to stay with made me feel as if he were a total stranger.

He kept repeating, "I'm going to go stay with friends, honey."

This puzzled me. He was calling me "honey," yet in the same sentence he was referring to people that I knew very well as if they were nameless and unknown.

The whole time Liam was doing this, he was still using sweet adjectives when he spoke. He had a strangely serene, robotic demeanor about him, except that he was sweating profusely.

Even with the sweat dripping down his face, Liam and I leaned over the pile of black garbage bags at the same time and kissed.

"I've got to get Hannah to her tennis tournament," I said. "We're running late."

"Okay, honey," he said. "I love you."

"I love you," I said right back.

Later, at Hannah's tennis tournament, I kept thinking about him telling me he loved me, and that I'd said it too. It was all so bizarre. I went to my car and called LeeAnn to see what time Liam had left. She told me that he'd left less than half an hour after I did. He took his clothes and everything in the closet, then went into the office, but came right back out. She said she'd stayed kind of close by. Observance distance.

Liam and I didn't have much contact before the next hearing. I had asked my attorney to hire a private investigator to take a picture, or somehow document the fact that Liam was living at his house in Tucson. I wanted to show the judge that Liam was lying to the court, and that he'd had a place to go all along. It took some convincing my attorney, Meghan, as she believed what Liam had told the judge. But Meghan finally consented, and we hired a private investigator to watch Liam's house.

Sure enough, a few days later, the P.I. had documentation and photos that Liam was indeed living at his home in Tucson. I had also told Meghan that I had a strong hunch that the rental contract Liam had produced for the court was for his studio/guest house, and not for the main house. A person would not know that unless they had been to his property, because both houses had the same address.

A couple of days before the hearing, I called Liam to ask how he was doing, and if there was anything that he wanted to talk about. Embittered, he said, "You had me one hundred percent." There was a pause before he continued: "You had all of me. I gave up everything for you. It's over now. If you have anything you want to offer, you can do it in writing and email it to me."

"Okay," I said. "Will you please bring me back my papers?"

"I didn't take"—and when he said the word "take," the pitch of his voice went up — "any papers," he said.

Once again, I could tell this conversation was going

nowhere, and my heart started to pound. I felt terrible for filing for divorce, yet at the same time, I was still upset that Liam had taken my papers and continued to lie about it. I was also panicked about the possibility of going bankrupt.

19

Eyewall

The second court hearing took place later that same month. Meghan had asked my accountant to be present, but he was not asked to testify, nor was he allowed to testify on my behalf. To my surprise, the judge told me that *I* had to testify. I had never done this before, and I found it extremely nerve-wracking.

When I gave my sworn testimony up on the witness stand, I felt like I had a mouthful of cotton, and I could hardly swallow. The courtroom was in the old part of the courthouse, which had no air conditioning; nevertheless, I was so cold that I was shivering and shaking. Whenever I'm nervous, I get cold. The judge asked me a bevy of questions about my various bank accounts, my trust, a partnership, why I'd withdrawn money from it at one point, and how much access I had to all of these different accounts. I told the judge that the only reason I'd pulled money out of the partnership account was because I was running out of money in my personal account, due to the fact that I was paying for everything for Liam and his family, including his children's education. I had promised my own son that I would help to pay for *his* college education, and the money in the partnership account was what I had been saving to use for that purpose.

As I was answering the judge's questions, Liam's attorney kept standing up and brandishing papers. "Well, what is this, then?" he spat at me, and with another shake of his wrist, "What is this?" I couldn't see because of the distance, and I shook my head, saying, "I don't know." Liam's attorney snapped back, "Well, your signature is on it, and you don't even know what it is? Don't you think you ought to know?" A couple of times the judge told him to stop interrupting and sit down.

Later, I realized that one of the papers was a photocopy of the stub from Liam's paychecks that I'd signed when I did the payroll for our farm employees. As my mom's Alzheimer's worsened, my parents had requested that I have power of attorney. I took this responsibility seriously and felt it was my duty to always do things as my mom would have done.

The judge also ordered me to pay Liam more than $3,500 per month in spousal support. Here I had spent the past five years paying for Liam's mortgages, flights, healthcare, phone plan, clothing, pickup truck, and salary, as well as his children's homes, cars, and college, and now I was being ordered by the court to give Liam more money. The spousal support was to continue indefinitely until Liam found a job. He had to document his search each week and submit it to the court, or he would lose the monthly spousal support. I was reminded of why so many people who have been through a divorce end up broke and bankrupt, with their lives destroyed.

Toward the end of the hearing, my attorney told the judge that she had surveillance video footage of Liam coming and going from his house in Tucson, and that he had not been truthful to the court when he'd claimed that he had nowhere to go. My lawyer also brought up the fact that after the last hearing, he'd refused to move back into the house, and she further speculated that his refusal was a control mechanism. You could see from the judge's face that she wasn't pleased. Looking right at my attorney, she announced "exclusive possession." My lawyer turned to me and said, "You got your house back." I breathed a deep sigh of relief, and felt an overwhelming sense of gratitude.

The judge and lawyers were ready to adjourn the hearing, but Liam still had the computer I'd bought for him to use. I whispered to my attorney that I wanted it back. She motioned to the judge and said, "One last thing, Your Honor. My client would like her computer returned by Mr. O'Connor." The judge turned to Liam and asked him right then and there to return my computer. Looking visibly upset, Liam said that he would first need to copy his files. I knew that if he left the courtroom with that computer, he was going to wipe it clean. My attorney asked if anyone had a memory stick, thumb drive, or CD so that he could copy the files, but nobody did. "In that case," the judge said to Liam, "back it up tonight and return the computer tomorrow."

That was the final item, and the hearing was adjourned.

The next morning, Liam came to the house at 9:30, as we had arranged in court. He had his own great big Apple twenty-inch computer that he'd left there in the office. I wondered why he had made such a fuss over keeping the Apple laptop I'd bought for him, unless there was something on it that he didn't want me to find. I had tried to use the big one, but he had put a password on it. He had given me a password the year before, but it was apparent that he had changed it since then, and this made it impossible for me to access the computer.

When Liam came into the house in his white linen shirt and faded blue jeans, we didn't say much to each other. He was acting standoffish. I started to reach out for his arm, but he quickly withdrew it. I could feel him recoil. Based on his mannerisms, I could tell he was already dating. I had also looked him up on the online dating service that we had met on just to see if he was on there.Sure enough, I found his profile. It made me feel sick to my stomach.

Liam packed up his great big computer and set the laptop on my desk. As he started to walk out the office door, he said, "There you are. There it is."

"Wait a minute," I said. "I want to make sure this computer is working. Why are there two users on it? The display looks entirely different."

Liam opened up a screen, pointed, and said tartly, "I have to show you how to open it? You are *here* with your name."

I knew I wasn't going to get anything from him. Just opening it up and briefly trying to navigate the system, it was obvious that Liam had done exactly what I had feared. He'd wiped the computer clean.

For several weeks after the hearing, each time we talked on the phone or exchanged emails, Liam would relentlessly accuse me of berating and abusing him in court, portraying himself as the victim, and yet I was the one who had been ordered to take the witness stand and undergo an interrogation. I was the one who had been questioned by the judge, as well as cross-exam-ined by Liam's attorney, who would wave papers at me, jump up and down, and negate each one of my answers. It would not be for several months that I would come to understand that my deep empathy for Liam, and the feeling that I was going insane during these confrontations, was a result of his masterful psychological manipulation. He was gaslighting me.

It was now October. Hannah was in her senior year of high school. She had tennis tournaments, harvest was in full swing, and I was trying to get through each day without Liam. I could not believe how hard it was not to see him. As nutty as it sounds, part of me started fantasizing about him coming back and knocking on the front door, holding all of my papers, and saying he was sorry, let's start over, and that he would get another job. The other part of me asked, *Then what would I do?* I was beginning to think that he didn't really want a job. How would I continue to support him and his family? I had this feeling that he would take both me and the farm under, and I would let him—all in the name of love.

Even through all of this, I still felt responsible for taking care of Liam. I told Meghan that I wanted to give him a lump sum for spousal support, rather than make the monthly payments until he got a job. I wanted to be good to him. If my dad or my friends knew, they would have thought that I had lost my mind. Even telling my attorney was hard. She wanted me to make him sweat it out and look for a job each day, recording all of his efforts for the judge. But I couldn't help myself. Meghan thought it was ludicrous to offer him $50,000, but I didn't care.

I knew that Liam had filed for unemployment, because as his past employer, I had received a letter from the Unemployment Insurance office asking me to either agree to or contest his request to receive unemployment benefits. Since he had signed the piece of paper at my dad's before he left for Tucson stating that he'd voluntarily quit, this prevented him from being entitled to any benefits. It was his idea to tell my dad that he was going to Tucson, and that he wasn't sure when he would be back. The Unemployment Insurance office sent me a copy of the paper that Liam had filled out and filed. On it he wrote that he was owed unemployment because, "he was tricked into signing the paper that said he was quitting."

I didn't think he'd been tricked. He quit. I did not contest it, but I did send in a copy of the paper he'd signed at my dad's house stating that he was resigning. Shortly thereafter, the Unemployment Insurance office sent me a letter informing me that they would pay Liam unemployment benefits, and they would not take it out of our farm's reserve account of payroll taxes that we retained with the state as an employer. They also added that he would be able to receive unemployment for ninety-nine weeks, much longer than the usual twenty-six weeks. After the recession of 2008, due to the flat recovery, Congress had extended the maximum benefits period to ninety-nine weeks. Liam benefited from the extra time.

My lawyer and Liam's lawyer negotiated back and forth a bit, and after they counteroffered with a lump sum of $75,000, we settled on $50,000. Meanwhile, time kept on ticking. It was November before my attorney was able to formally submit our agreement to the court.

The first Friday of every month, Hannah's parochial high school class attended mass at eleven in the morning. On the first Friday of November, I joined the service along with Hannah's classmates and their parents. As I sat there in the pews of the same Catholic parish I'd attended in elementary and high school, asking God to forgive me for winding up in yet another marriage mess, I realized that I needed to forgive Liam. It was God's gracious mercy in forgiving me that had brought me to this conclusion. Life truly is about forgiveness, and I decided that I was going to call Liam and tell him that I forgave him for taking the papers from my Almond Timeline. This wasn't about my feelings, it was about moving forward.

That evening, Hannah and I were at home watching TV, and as she was doing her homework, we started talking about getting ready for Thanksgiving. The more we talked, the more inconsolable Hannah became about Liam's daughter and family not being there for what would have been our sixth Thanksgiving together. Hannah liked Sherrie and the little grandkids. She also liked Liam. Through her tears, she asked me, "Why did Liam leave? Why did all of this happen, Mom? Can't you forgive him for taking those papers?"

I couldn't believe it. I told Hannah how I'd had that very same thought earlier in the day. "I'm so sorry, angel," I said. "I don't want another divorce. I see how hard this is for you, too. I'm going to call Liam and tell him I forgive him and ask him to please come back." I wiped away Hannah's tears and hugged her.

In the years right after my first divorce, I realized that forgiveness doesn't necessarily mean that whatever the other person did that hurt you is okay. Rather, forgiveness means letting go and accepting reality. I forgave my first husband for his contempt toward me, and I forgave my ex-mother-in-law for being so intrusive. Since then, it has felt good to be free of the discord between us. Moreover, Dale, his mother, and I are now all good friends.

Back to forgiving Liam. I didn't call him right away, but we had already been emailing back and forth. His emails cut like knives. They were filled with long paragraphs about how selfish he thought I was. He wrote that he'd tried to protect me from my senile father, who had destroyed what we had, and that my father was the worst person he had ever met. In another email, Liam wrote that he'd tried to protect me from my maniacal ex-husband and spoiled children, and in another, he wrote that he'd done everything for me and given up everything for me. How could I be so cruel as to choose my father, money, possessions, and children's inheritance over him and our marriage?

I wanted to just forget about the past and move forward. In fact, when I wrote Liam back, I ignored the hateful and hurtful emails he'd sent, and asked if we could reconcile and call a truce. I had read about other couples reconciling even in the midst of their divorce. "Please come back," I wrote in my email. "Let's be together like before, like we were. There is no difference between then and now."

"No difference?" he wrote back. "Back then, when you threw me out and filed for divorce? I loved you then, and love you today, however I will not be put in a position to be abused. I don't ever want to be back in court to be falsely accused, berated, or mistreated."

In a subsequent phone call, Liam said, "If you want to reconcile and get back together again, then we're each going to have to give the other one half of what we own. It's not about what is equal, it's about giving the other person half of what they have."

Liam went on: "I will not be put in that position again, where I could be thrown out of the house, onto the street, on my ear, and be left with nothing. I won't take that risk again."

I was devastated. I couldn't believe that Liam was putting what seemed like a price tag on us getting back together again. He was using my desire for reconciliation as a bargaining chip, and the land and assets as collateral. I wanted to reconcile— oh, how I wanted to—yet at the same time, I felt that if I did, it would be a breach of the trust my family had placed in me.

Sometimes during the day, I missed Liam so much that it physically hurt. At times, it felt like every part of me was going to come out of my skin, as if I was going to explode. Other times, it felt like I was going to implode, as if the air around me was so heavy that I could collapse inward and self-destruct.

I wondered if this was how someone who cut themselves might feel. I would never do that, but I could see how it might temporarily displace the hurt. I also wondered if this was how someone who takes their own life might feel, because they would do anything to stop the unbearable pain. I would never commit suicide, either, because I believe my life is a gift from God and not mine to take, but in my deep despair, I garnered compassion for those who had lost all hope and felt they had no other way to stop their pain. Some days I didn't think I was going to make it.

I kept thinking about what I should do, and what was at stake. I pondered the big questions: What does it mean to love someone? At what point do you give them everything you have? How much do you give of yourself? If you give all of yourself, how can you replenish yourself to be able to continue to give?

I also considered the many sacrifices my dad and mom had made, and how hard they had worked to make the land productive. Unsure of what to do, I called Eleanor, my mom's best friend, and asked if I could talk to her in person. "Come on over," she said. As we sat in the stately yet comfortable library in her house designed by a noted Modernist architect, with framed photos covering an entire wall from floor to ceiling, including some of her with my mom, she told me how she had seen my mom forsake many comforts to help my dad build the farm. My mom's income had helped them to buy more land. She said she knew that my mom would have wanted the land to go to Cody and Hannah, to blood. It felt as though my mom were speaking through her best friend. Eleanor reinforced what my better instincts had already told me, but her affirmation gave me the resoluteness that I needed.

When I got back to my house, I sent Liam an email saying that the land was not mine to give or divide, that it was my parents' land, and I was just the vessel, the means by which to carry it on to the next generation. He replied with the same inflexibility he'd shown in previous emails. "Sign over half of the land, or we go our separate ways," he wrote.

A week later, on the Saturday before Thanksgiving, I had breakfast with my dad and Charlotte. As we ate blueberry pancakes, I told them about what was happening between me and Liam. With every bite, I grew more and more despondent. The thought of being without Liam was unbearable. I felt a deep, interminable longing for him with every ounce of my physical being. Later that morning, back at my house, I picked up the phone and called him. Contrary to my better instincts, I told Liam that I was sorry, and that I forgave him for taking my papers. "Please come back," I begged him. "And it can be like it was before."

"Well, put the money in my account," he said.

I thought he meant the spousal support check, and even though I knew it was a little early, I had the money, and so I told him I would.

We hung up, and I figured I'd do the bank transaction that Monday.

A couple of hours later, Liam called back. "I just checked my bank account," he said, "and the money's not there. I don't see where you made a deposit."

His tone was menacing, as if he were a kidnapper telling the victim's family where to deposit the ransom.

"What are you talking about?" I said. "I was going to go to the bank on Monday."

"For someone who sounded so serious about getting back together," Liam continued in a callous tone, "you'd think they would have done what they said they were going to do."

I could not believe what I was hearing. In a flash, my mouth felt so dry that I could hardly talk; my ears were ringing, and I started to shake. "Are you talking about the spousal support? That's what I was going to put in this week."

"If you're serious about getting back together, put $25,000 in my account, and I'll buy an airline ticket and be home for Thanksgiving, so we can be a family again. Think about the little grandkids, especially Colleen."

I just kept saying his name. *Liam, Liam.* I didn't know what else to say, my heart was pounding in my ears. I had so many thoughts and emotions slamming me at one time, and my mind was a blur. I thought I was going to faint. He asked if I was going to do it, and I said I didn't know that was what he meant. I told him I thought he was talking about the spousal support, not the lump sum payment.

"If you came back, you would live here and I'd pay for everything like before, so why would you need the $25,000 if we're going to get back together?"

"I knew you weren't built that way," Liam said with spite.

"Built that way?" I repeated. "What does that mean?"

"You don't have it in you to do the right thing. Think about it. I'm going now," he said, and hung up the phone.

The anguish I felt was so unbearable that I went outside and screamed: a blood-curdling scream. It felt as though someone had stuck a knife in my heart. I could not believe Liam wanted the same amount of money to come back as I was supposed to give him in the divorce. I was starting to think maybe he had a gambling problem, and still, regardless of all this, I desperately wanted to see him.

In a flurry of subsequent emails, Liam continued to demand the cash, insisting that if I loved him, I'd send him the $25,000 and sign over half of everything I owned to him. By that Friday night, when Hannah had gone to her dad's for the weekend, I was so distraught that I decided to go to church. I drove into town, but the church was locked. Feeling desperate, I drove across town to a convent where an order of cloistered nuns lived, nuns who had been there since I was in high school. They lived in a whitewashed brick building inside a high-walled, plaza-style courtyard. As I entered through the double doors of the scrolled wrought-iron gate, I saw a huge wooden cross in the middle of the plaza, which was surrounded by grass. There were symmetrical walkways and climbing red roses growing over the walls. I walked up the wide, terraced steps to the front door in tears. I rang the doorbell and asked if I could please talk to someone. The Mother Superior, whose native language was French, came out from the religious community's private quarters, and we sat in the foyer. I talked and cried nonstop for forty minutes, practically wringing my hands, explaining my situation and asking her what I should do.

With a contagious peacefulness, she looked at me, and the very first words she spoke were in the form of a question. "How do you know he will come back if you give him that money?"

Her question felt like the most profound thing I had ever heard. For some reason, this sweet, soft-spoken nun named Bernadette, whom I wasn't even sure could understand me because I was crying so hard, had spoken the hard truth I needed to hear. I believe the Holy Spirit was with us and helped Mother Bernadette to miraculously get through to me. For a fleeting moment, I saw Liam's deception. Could it be that he had no intention of coming back, and it was only a ploy to get the money? It was hard for me to comprehend, as I was still dying to see him, but the veil of illusion was starting to lift.

The week before Christmas, Liam and I were going back and forth on email about halving our property. He added that if I put $25,000 in his bank account, he would be able to be home for Christmas. As irrational as it seems, I still felt overcome by a desire, an insatiable craving, to see Liam and be with him again. So I called him.

"Why are you doing this?" I said.

"I knew you weren't built that way," he said. "If you can't halve our properties, you'll have to go your way and I'll go mine, and we'll start dating other people. You decide."

For the rest of that day, I paced the floor of my house, agonizing over which choice to make. I could hardly function. I loved Liam so much, and yet to sign over half of what I owned would be selling out what my mom and dad had worked so hard to build. It all seemed surreal. In my first marriage, I'd fought not to lose my kids, and now with this marriage, I was in a fight not to lose my land.

As the day dragged on, it became clear to me what I had to do. I didn't want to, but I knew that it meant my survival and my livelihood. The next morning, I went to my computer and sent Liam an email stating that he was right, I was not, in his words, "built that way." I could not sign over to him half of everything I owned, and I could not put the $25,000 in his account for an airline ticket. He would have to go his way, and I would go mine. I didn't want to go through more pain of knowing I would not be able to see him again, but to me the simplest and best way to end this standoff, which is what it had become, was to call his bluff. End it the way he said to end it, if I didn't comply with his demands. I was shaking as I hit the Send button.

My attorney, Meghan, was still working on documents for my case, hammering out the details of the lump sum settlement and a few other details about tools Liam wanted to pick up from my garage. That was fine with me. I secretly thought that if I kept the tools, I could see Liam when he came to get them.

I called Meghan and asked her to please finish the paper-work, and not drag it out any longer. She had been busy on another case, which at the time I felt worked to my advan-tage, because I was not ready, mentally or emotionally, for the divorce to be finalized. I probably never would be ready, but I knew then that it had to be done.

The next day, Meghan sent the final settlement agreement to Liam's attorney, who then faxed it to Liam in Tucson. Liam signed the agreement and faxed it back in acceptance of the terms: I would give him $50,000 in spousal support, to be divided into two separate payments of $25,000 each.

The following day, I went to Meghan's office to sign the paperwork. On the way, I stopped at my bank to get the cashier's check required for the first lump sum payment of $25,000. The head cashier, Kathy, whom I knew from my frequent visits to the bank, was patient and friendly as I stood at her teller window, sobbing and crying. Tears poured down my face as I told her this was money that I was paying my husband, whom I was divorcing.

"This is crazy," I told Kathy. "I'm divorcing someone who I'm so in love with. But I have to do it."

Kathy nodded in agreement. "You do have to do it," she said. "Be strong."

At that moment, I knew I had to stop the bleeding.

When I got back to my attorney's office with the cashier's check, the divorce agreement was finalized. Those last conver-sations with Liam, when he'd demanded that I put $25,000 in his account so he could fly home first for Thanksgiving, then for Christmas, had left me feeling dirty and icky. He was the user, and I was his pawn. It was finally sinking in that in the mirage I was experiencing with Liam, he used money as a form of leverage. I felt like I was in a fog. It was all I could do to get through each day, sometimes even just an hour at a time. I felt like I was moving in slow motion. I couldn't focus or concentrate on anything. Each day, I had to force myself to get out of bed and get to my dad's to pay the bills and take care of the business. It was a painful struggle. Sometimes I would just break down and cry uncontrollably.

Around the same time, I called my close girlfriends, whom I had always cherished but had kept at bay during the love storm with Liam. When we were married, if I voiced wanting to see my friends, Liam would always say, "Don't you think I want to see my friends too? I'm out here in California, slaving for your dad." Liam made me feel guilty for even wanting to see them. In retrospect, I realize he was trying to isolate me from my friends and family. So, when I told my girlfriends about the divorce, they were not as surprised as I thought they might have been.

20

Rope Tornado

The next month, I sent Liam the second lump sum payment of $25,000, and my monetary obligations were fulfilled. It was around this same time, in January, that I learned my therapist, Dr. Rose, was retiring. She recommended that rather than continue to see another forensic psychologist like herself, that instead I see an expert in pathological love relationships. I had to look up the word "pathological" in the dictionary, because I didn't know exactly what it meant. At the same time Dr. Rose kept throwing out the term "sociopath," which I also had to look up in the dictionary, because I didn't understand the difference between the two words.

Dr. Rose gave me the phone number of an institute that specialized in pathological love relationships. I was perturbed that she'd referred me there in the first place, but because I valued her expertise, I reluctantly followed up. Upon contacting the institute, I was asked to fill out a lengthy written assessment of my marriage to Liam. Their intake department determined that my marriage fit the definition of a pathological love relationship. Even though I doubted their conclusion, which seemed far-fetched, I started having weekly phone consultations with one of their counselors, who was based on the East Coast. During our 6:00 a.m. sessions, she would educate me as to the difficulties in recognizing a sociopath, and she also recommended several books, including *The Sociopath Next Door*, which I begrudgingly read. I was astounded to see similarities with Liam's behavior, and I started listening to the counselor a little more intently. She also explained that Liam had a type of personality disorder known as "Cluster B." His most pronounced symptom, she said, was narcissism. But even after six months of intensive counseling and reading all of the literature that had been recommended, I still found it hard to believe that Liam was actually a sociopath, and that this could have happened to me. Because, after all, they didn't know Liam like I knew Liam. No matter what the counselor said, I couldn't imagine him being mean to me on purpose.

Uncertain as I was, I wanted to seek another professional opinion. I remembered Patricia Evans, the author of five books on verbal abuse and controlling behavior, whom I had consulted during my first divorce. My attorney at the time had suggested that I attend one of Patricia's retreats on clarity in relationships, and it had helped me to unpack the unhealthy relationship dynamic in my first marriage. I decided to reach out to Patricia again, even though I wasn't sure if she would remember me from the retreat. I called and told her about my current situation, and she was quick to identify the financial abuse I had gone through with Liam. She was also curious about his past marriages, and encouraged me to contact his previous wives.

"Why don't you give one of them a call," she said.

"Oh, no, I couldn't do that!"

"Why not?" Patricia asked.

"I just couldn't."

"Why not?" she repeated.

"I don't really know why," I said. I paused and thought for a second, then continued, "For starters, I have no idea how to get a hold of them. I don't even know their last names, never mind that they live in three different states. I also don't feel comfortable calling them, because I have no reason not to believe Liam's story that they're all crazy."

"Even if you believe him," Patricia said, "wouldn't it be nice to commiserate with another woman who has shared your feelings? Maybe she could tell you things that would help to reconcile this in your heart and mind. You could console and empathize with one another. Comfort each other. Be a friend."

I heard Patricia's words, but at the time, it was too much of a stretch for me to imagine tracking down Liam's ex-wives and calling them.

At the beginning of February, after I'd spoken with Patricia, Liam emailed to ask if I could send him the guitar I'd bought him for his birthday a few years earlier. It was a signed Steve Miller guitar, hand-painted with a boy and a girl square-dancing along a white picket fence, and a dog howling in the foreground with a big yellow moon shining above them all. When I bought the guitar, I was so excited I'd found it, because it reminded me of the card Liam had sent after our first date, as well as the Steve Miller song he'd referenced in an email before we got married.

In the court documents, Liam had asked for the guitar, along with the tools in the garage. I agreed to give it back to him, and when I started wrapping the guitar in bubble wrap, getting it ready to ship, I was flooded with memories of how happy I'd felt when I'd bought it for him. Tears streamed down my face.

I suppose some would have been relieved that it was all over, but I still felt huge holes in my heart. The only consolation I knew of was *time*. Because of my first divorce, I knew that time would eventually heal these wounds. How big the scars would be, I did not know, but I knew that a mile begins with one step. Each night when I went to bed, I told myself, was one teeny, tiny step toward healing. I knew that as sure as the sun would come up the next day, I was guaranteed another step; even if it was a microscopic step, it was still movement forward. That was how I got through the pain. Another way was by writing down the reasons I had divorced Liam. I wrote them down on index cards and kept the cards on my nightstand. I did this to remind myself of his unethical and immoral character. Nighttime was always the worst; it was when I second-guessed myself and felt the most alone. I would read the cards in order to reassure myself that I had done the right thing.

Come Valentine's Day, Liam sent me another email. When I saw his name in my inbox, I felt a rush of adrenaline, my face flushed, my heart started pounding, and my hands felt numb and tingly. I sat there looking at his name on the computer screen. I thought about deleting the message and not even opening it, but I couldn't resist. As my heart pounded harder, I clicked on the email and read it.

Liam wrote, "Even though I am without a Valentine, I hope you have found comfort in the arms of another." I resisted emailing him back, even though I wanted to. His pull was still magnetic. I wasn't dating, and I couldn't even think about it, but I was realizing that even though I might want something, it didn't mean I could have it, or that it was good for me. I thought about Bonnie and Clyde. I thought about Patty Hearst and Stockholm syndrome. I would have done anything for Liam.

I finally understood that I had been brainwashed.

Over the next few months, Liam continued to send sporadic emails. When Easter came, he wrote me a long, rambling letter professing his religious faith and updating me on the birth of a new grandchild. I still trembled with anticipation before I opened it, but once I read the words, I no longer felt the same intense longing for Liam. Instead, I felt an aversion. To my astonishment, my unquenchable desire to see Liam had begun to subside.

In June, he sent more emails, and was now back to demanding the tools. I had not replied to any of his previous emails, but as per my attorney's instructions, I did reply to these. He sent email after email demanding that I send him a list of the tools in the garage. I thought that if he couldn't remember what tools were there, and didn't even know which ones he needed, why should I send him a list? My lawyer did not want him coming to get them at my house, so she suggested that I rent a storage facility and tell him that I would pay for one month, and that he was to pick them up there. After that, he could pay for the storage, or the tools would be confiscated. A week later, the foreman on our farm helped me to move all the tools to a storage unit. Every day I checked to see if Liam had picked them up, because as demented as it sounds, I was still hoping to run into him. Luckily, for the sake of my recovery, I never did. One day the tools were there, and the next day they were gone.

A month later, in July, I went to get the mail out of the mailbox in front of my house. I couldn't believe it when I saw a letter from Liam. I was so excited. This was the first time he had ever sent me a real letter in the mail. I ran inside and opened it. The letter started out by saying that in lieu of "missing equipment" that wasn't in the storage unit, which he could have used to earn money, and with his unemployment benefits running out, he was having difficulty surviving. He also wrote that due to his age, because I'd caused him to lose his job and he'd been forced to work in agriculture for the past five years, he was having a hard time finding a job and making ends meet. He asked if I could help him survive by sending a check to pay off one of his home mortgages, in the amount of $6,084. He had even included a payment slip from the company, he said, "for my convenience." The letter ended by saying, "I know this would be a sacrifice on your part. I would be grateful if you could see your way to do this."

That last line would have worked a while back. I'd have jumped at the chance to help Liam, given anything to rescue him, but now I was experiencing a different sensation. His letter didn't elicit the sympathy that it would have in earlier days. Instead, it made me disbelieving of his circumstances.

I knew he was lying about his unemployment benefits running out. As his former employer, I had received the same letter from the state as he had, a blind copy, confirming that he was receiving the ninety-nine weeks of extended benefits. I also knew that he had his own enormous supply of equipment and tools in Tucson, if he really wanted to work and earn money. He didn't need the tools that I had purchased for the farm. I had already noticed on his online dating profile that he'd listed his profession as "handyman," which made me sick. I knew this had sexual connotations. He was using his handyman skills as a tool of seduction.

That was the final straw. Instead of wanting to save Liam, now I wanted to know the whole story behind him. Who was he? What was the deal? I remembered what Patricia Evans had told me: "Why don't you contact his ex-wives?" I could almost hear her saying, "Find them, talk to them."

And so I did.

21

Calm

It was Thursday evening, July 5, 2012. I was sitting on my bed, cross-legged, hunched over, clenching my cell phone and pressing it to my ear as hard as I could. My head was spinning. I was listening to every word she was saying, and I couldn't get enough. I had so many questions. I needed to hear more.

We talked for two-and-a-half hours. The realization came on slowly. It was hard to wrap my head around everything she was telling me at one time. I couldn't absorb it. Earlier in the day, for two hours, I had searched online for her number. I had compiled a list of twelve numbers that were related to the name Janet Keller, who I knew was Liam's third wife. I called every single one. Some were disconnected or not in service, some were wrong numbers, and with some, the phone now belonged to someone else. But I kept trying. Unbelievably, it was the very last number I called that finally connected me with someone who knew Janet. I was ecstatic. All I knew was what Liam had told me: that she did alterations in a men's tailor shop.

The woman who answered the phone was hesitant to give me Janet's actual phone number, but after I explained that I was going through an emotionally distressing time, and was hoping Janet could help me, she relented.

I was so nervous I was shaking. I sat with the phone in my hand for about forty-five minutes. On a piece of paper, I wrote down what I was going to say, scratched it out, wrote and rewrote it, then finally I had it. I called the number. There was no answer, only Janet's recorded voice saying to leave a message after the beep.

As I started to leave my message, I could hardly hear myself talk because the pounding in my ears was so loud, and my heart felt like it was going to surge right out of my chest. I began slowly. "My name is Virginia Bennett," I said. "And I was married to Liam O'Connor for five years. We are now divorced, and I'm trying to recover financially and emotionally, and I was wondering if you would be willing to share any information or insight about your experience." After I left my cell phone number, I hung up and waited. I sat on my bed with the phone in my hand for an hour and a half, and then she called.

Janet didn't stop talking for the first forty-five minutes—and I didn't stop her, either. She started out describing a fairy tale. The very first thing she said was, "He treated me like a princess. He put me on a pedestal. He swept me off my feet, and we were engaged in three months. He bought me the biggest diamond ring I had ever seen."

When she said this, all I could think about was how I had bought and paid for our wedding rings myself, and his remark that "we're not jewelry people." And that was after waiting two long, arduous years and "building a foundation," as Liam liked to say. What a farce. Our foundation was not strong at all. It was made of sand. Quicksand.

Janet told me that they'd had a big wedding, she had become Mormon, and they were sealed in the Mormon Temple. To be "sealed" meant to participate in a special ceremony ensuring that a couple would be together in the afterlife. All I could think of was how plain and simple our marriage ceremony had been. There was no mention of me becoming Mormon until the end.

Janet went on to tell me about how she'd had her own business, a high-end men's tailoring shop, where she'd made custom suits and shirts. She'd also made costumes on set for the movie industry. After a year of marriage, Liam had quit his job and persuaded her to sell her business, claiming that he could make far more money in the stock market with the proceeds. It sounded familiar; toward the end of our marriage, Liam had mentioned his investment savvy. All I could think about was how he had done the same thing with me, quitting his job seven months after we'd been married. He'd also told Janet he would take care of paying all the bills, and she didn't have to worry about anything. He'd told her to put all the bills on his desk, and he would deal with them. As time went on, he told her that he was losing money, and he made her believe that they were in deep financial trouble. Liam said he would have to sell their Steinway grand piano. He told her she had better go back to work. Janet went back to her shop, which she had sold to a friend, and worked there for a while, until she started getting calls from credit card companies and bill collectors saying that she was behind in her payments. When Janet asked Liam about it, he said, "Well, if you would stop giving me these bills to pay. You keep putting them on my desk and expect me to take care of them." She found out that he wasn't paying the bills at all, and that he was using her money for other things. He'd racked up $65,000 in debt in her name. He was throwing money around everywhere, using her credit cards to remodel his house in Tucson.

I thought back to how he'd told me about all the remodeling he'd done in that beautiful house. It was no wonder the colors were soft pastels. Janet had chosen them, not Liam, as he had led me to believe. I also thought about how he was a master at turning things around, claiming that he was the one who was being hurt and abused, when in fact he was the abuser.

Janet told me that Liam was always kind and supportive of her visiting her aunt in Florida. He would encourage her to go there and spend time with her, especially when things were just beginning to get stressful with the money situation. One time in particular, he drove her to the airport, and on the way, he said, "Oh, we're going to make a quick stop at an office. We need to take out a second mortgage on the house." After the divorce, Janet found out that this stop on the way to the airport was not to sign paperwork to take out a second mortgage, but rather to sign paperwork that relinquished her half of the ownership of the house, giving Liam full ownership. The meeting had been staged. By the time they got the divorce, it was too late to do anything. The time period to contest something like that had already passed. All I could think about was how Liam had lied to me about taking the papers from my Almond Timeline, and I wondered what other personal business matters he might have lied about in *our* future.

Janet told me that at the end of their marriage, he would pack up her things in the middle of the night, then the next day say to her, "Why are you still here?" She said she asked him, "Where am I supposed to go?" He had racked up all of her credit cards and persuaded her to sell her once-profitable business. She had to file for bankruptcy. She had no money, no business, no car, and no credit left, nothing.

Liam eventually went back to work, and when he was gone for a few days, she packed up all of her things. She got her brother to help her put the furniture, throw rugs, artwork, and paintings into a truck. Everything in the house was hers— things that either she had bought, or Liam had bought using her credit cards. Everything except for his guitars, that is. She moved in with her mother and started to build her life back again.

I thought about Liam's version of events. He'd told me that he'd come home from a business trip to find that Janet had taken everything, leaving him with nothing except for his guitars, and how he had gotten down on his knees and said, "Thank you, Jesus." He had made me feel so sorry for him, telling me that she was crazy. I could see now that she wasn't crazy at all. She'd had to leave for her survival and livelihood. Just like me.

Janet told me that for a long time she still believed in the same dream Liam had "designed" for her at the beginning of their relationship. After the divorce, it took her six years to finally let go and realize it had been a fantasy. It was all part of his trap. She told me he'd tried to make her think she was cruel, selfish, abusive, and unloving toward him. Liam had tried to make me think I was those exact same things, too: cruel, selfish, abusive, and unloving toward him. He'd gaslighted both of us.

As the conversation ended, I said, "Janet, thank you so very, very much for calling me back. You didn't have to, but you did, and by sharing your experience, you've helped me solve the mystery of Liam."

When I said goodbye, I was still sitting cross-legged on the bed. I couldn't move. I sat there, thinking about everything Janet had told me.

The next day, I felt inspired to speak with another one of

Liam's ex-wives. My conversation with Janet had been trans-
formative; it had completely shifted my perspective and
unlocked my brain. I went online and did the same research as
I'd done for her, and in a couple of hours, I was able to find a
number for someone whose name sounded like Liam's second
wife, Kimberly. Liam never gave me last names, so I had to
pay a fee to find hers through a marriage records search, as
I had done with Janet. When I finally got her on the phone
and introduced myself, right away she put me at ease with her
sense of humor. "What number are you?" she asked. I laughed
and told her I was number four. Then she said, "How about
that voice of his? Smooth as honey." I knew exactly what she
meant. We went on to talk for half an hour, during which time
she further confirmed that Liam was a chameleon who could
change his colors based on his surroundings. With her, he had
been a beer-guzzling, earringed Harley-Davidson rider, ape
hangers on his bike and all. I couldn't believe it; it was such a
different persona from what he had presented to me.

After that call, two out of three ex-wives was enough for me
to see the pattern.

Talking to Liam's ex-wives made me think about the movie
Black Widow, which starred Debra Winger and came out in
1987. Toward the end of my marriage to Liam, somehow
this movie had come up in conversation. I didn't think much
about the film, other than that I liked the actors and thought
the premise was interesting. I asked Liam if he had seen it. He
didn't say anything. I wasn't sure if he'd heard me or not, so
I asked again, this time looking directly at him. I got a half
yes, with the familiar quick nod of his head at an angle, and a
shrug of his shoulders. At the time, I thought it was kind of a
weird reply. Either you've seen a movie, or you haven't. Why
wouldn't he answer me?

What was interesting, I later realized, was the irony of my new understanding of Liam as it related to the movie. The main character was a female gold digger who was confident and charming, and could masterfully seduce and win over any man. Once she had picked him out, she would research her wealthy lover's interests, then tailor her own interests to match his. She became an imposter, changing her persona and character to suit her lover's personality. After marrying and killing her victim, she would inherit his money. In the movie, she did this three times, before she was finally caught by a federal agent.

After talking with Liam's ex-wives, I noted something even more striking: within four months of meeting Liam, both me and my dad had been bitten by a black widow spider. It's uncanny that the name of the black widow spider, *Latrodectus mactans*, a mixture of Latin and Greek, means "deadly biting robber." Not only is the black widow a creepy spider, it is also a spider whose name denotes exactly what happened to me after meeting Liam. While the relationship didn't kill me, as I'm here to tell my story, it inflicted poisonous emotional wounds and robbed me of my intellectual property.

I finally came to the disturbing conclusion that Liam was a master of disguise, an imposter. He became a reflection of my interests in order to control my purse strings. At the beginning of our relationship, he'd also used what I had told him about my ex, Dale, to create his new persona. He made a big point of reminding me of how he was everything that Dale was not. Early on, I took Liam's comment, "If I could wave a magic wand…" to heart.

He waved it alright, spreading pixie dust so thick I got lost in a cloud of lust.

Liam's painstaking way of making me feel that his dreams were my dreams, that his goals were my goals, and that his financial interests were my financial interests, was all part of his conditioning me to trust him unreservedly. Trust is what made me feel safe with him. Like Debra Winger's character in the movie *Black Widow*, Liam purposefully designed the dream to meet his love interest's interests. The dream felt so real to me, but in fact, it was not. It was a fantasy that Liam had created. He tailored the dream to whomever he was trying to catch in his web. The fact that Liam's dreams and goals were similar to mine was not by chance, as it would be in an ethical or non-pathological relationship. Liam's dreams and goals were plotted and crafted. Just like his last wife had said, he designed them.

I have often wondered: at what point does a person realize they are being brainwashed and could potentially be in danger? I was completely brainwashed for years and didn't know it. The process was slow and undetectable. Like a frog placed in water that's slowly heated up. If you put a frog into a pot of boiling water, the frog will jump right out to escape the danger. But if you set the frog in water that is cool and pleasant, and the water heats up slowly, the frog will become tranquil and unaware of the threat until it is too late. Since the frog's instincts are geared toward detecting sudden changes, it will eventually die, unable to save itself. Humans are this way, too, sometimes. Unaware of a slowly developing threat, we can become complacent and relaxed, until we find ourselves in serious hot water.

In retrospect, I felt my soul was slowly dying when I was with Liam. So slowly that it was hard to detect exactly what posed a threat. I was blinded by the frenetic euphoria that his being and his body brought me. It wasn't until he left at the end of our marriage and moved back to Tucson that I was able to identify that the unbearable pains my body was suffering were actual withdrawal symptoms. Just as a heroin addict experiences excruciating pain when he stops taking heroin, I was experiencing the same thing, only my drug was Liam. That rush of euphoria I felt every time I was with him caused an increase in the dopamine levels in my brain, which rewarded and motivated me to be with him. I knew it wasn't right, that it was an addiction on a physical level, but he had a power over me.

Liam understood the value of his physical gifts. He was a master at using his sexual charisma to lure his prey. He knew just how to tailor his words and communication style to inspire love and devotion from women. He was also a master manipulator who maintained control by the act of withholding. The same way a drug dealer knows how to get someone hooked on drugs, Liam knew how to get women hooked on him. He knew how to bring someone to the brink, then let go, leaving them begging for more. I realized by that point that I had to go cold turkey. I could not see Liam, or, like a drug addict, I could relapse.

I had to use every ounce of willpower I could muster to disengage myself from him. He'd sucked me into a vortex. It's pretty hard to extricate something from a whirling vortex, but somehow, I made it out.

All that I gave him was never enough. He exploited my giving like a leech. I had also begun to feel like I was married to a gigolo, a young man paid or financially supported by an older woman to be her escort or lover. Only I wasn't an older woman. I was a couple of years younger, actually, but I still couldn't get the thought out of my head, and I felt mortified. I knew this was not how I was brought up. My parents had taught me the value of sharing one's life with a team player.

Toward the end of the marriage, and during the divorce, when Liam went after my dad, it made me feel deeply protective of the man who had raised me. Looking back, this was when things really started to fracture. Liam was going after a person who had been *my* protector. And my instincts to protect my dad were what ultimately protected me from being completely snowed by Liam, and losing everything in an avalanche.

It wasn't until I finally spoke to Liam's exes that I connected the dots. None of us had ever met or spoken to one another before. It was only by talking to his second and third wives that I uncovered his pattern of masquerading. Had I not spoken with them, we would have remained isolated from one another, our identities concealed, just as Liam had intended. Talking to Janet, especially, gave me the truth and validation I needed to be set free. To have the spell broken. It was the striking similarities and coincidences of sharing our lives for a while with a con artist that helped me to regain my composure. I knew I was not alone. Janet eventually got her life back, with a lot of hard work and perseverance. She told me that she had recently overcome stage 3 breast cancer, a double mastectomy, and had regained her successful career, tailoring clothing for a popular television series, as well as for several Oscar-nominated films. The discovery helped to alleviate my pain, and I felt very fortunate to have solved a mystery. Although to the experts, there was no mystery whatsoever.

They had tried to tell me all along, but until I could speak with someone else who'd had the same experiences, I just could not call Liam what he was: a white-collar sociopath. All the back-and-forth in the beginning of our relationship, for example, when he would call me and break it off, then call me back three days later as if nothing had happened, was part of his tactic of reeling me in, only to release me shortly thereafter. Liam's vacillation created a kind of hyped-up love, which was inevitably followed by a big letdown. The push and pull intensified my attraction, and in hindsight, I believe he knew exactly what he was doing. His moves were calculated.

Liam made me feel like a girl pulling the petals off a daisy flower, saying, "He loves me, he loves me not..." The problem was that this caused me to want to prove my love and loyalty even more; I wanted to show Liam that I would always be there for him. He would throw out bread crumbs, or dangle a carrot, always just enough to keep me hanging on. The calm, cool, collected demeanor I had at first found so impressive was really a sign that something was not right. Liam showed no outward emotional behavior in highly charged emotional situations, as if he were just an empty shell. For example, after the first court hearing, when the judge granted him permission to move back in, he calmly threw his clothes into plastic garbage bags, as if we hadn't just been in a contentious divorce hearing. He was completely serene and detached. He was talking to me, calling me "honey" and "babe," as if nothing had happened. He lacked empathy toward those who helped him, and believed that he could do no wrong. His love was not unconditional, as I knew love to be; his love was about compliance and obedience.

In working with the pathological relationship counselor, I learned how and why these men choose their victims. Sociopaths often target educated, high-achieving women with successful careers; women who are dependable and trusting of others, such as teachers, nurses, or CEOs. These types of men are often drawn toward overly empathetic women who will provide for their needs. They play the victim so as to elicit sympathy from their partners. Sociopaths feign compassion and empathy for others, but their sole concern is really themselves. In reality, their compassion is a kind of tactic, not a genuine expression of care. They can appear compassionate, but as with Liam, what they say and what they do are two different things.

I learned from the counselor how to recognize that someone might not be a trustworthy partner, or a mentally healthy person. The chemistry I felt with Liam was real, but the magical reality that he created was not. It was a fairy tale. At first this was such a depressing thought. How would I ever know what was real and what was not in my future relationships? But that is where the counselor helped me to understand how some of my own personality traits had made me vulnerable to this type of a man. I recognized that I was overly trusting and excessively empathetic, as well as loyal to a fault, thus preventing me from seeing Liam for the predator that he was. Some virtues can be a detriment. Mine had worked against me, but by seeing that, I could make better choices in the future.

These counseling sessions brought out things in me that I did not like to face in myself. It hurt to arrive at this depth of self-knowledge, but I wasn't going to let myself wallow anymore, or fret over what I'd done wrong. Once again, I'd let my children down and made a lot of trouble for my parents; I felt like a failure. I had to analyze the relationship and tear it all apart and examine the whole thing, which was a raw and painful process. This helped me to transform what had been a devastating experience into a tangible, factual, truthful, and real thing that I could then examine with others and no longer be afraid to call what it was: a pathological relationship. I was able to bring the experience out of the dark and into the light.

The first part of my healing process was to understand Liam's psychopathology, and to know that I was not alone in experiencing this type of relationship. The second part required me to work on letting go of the overpowering fear that I experienced being without him, and without my records of the farm. I had to dig into the recesses of my inner being for strength and faith in better days ahead, and believe in myself. I had to remember that I was competent and resourceful, and that I could get along without the silent messianic force that was Liam.

Beware, because as Dr. Rose once told me, the devil too can quote scripture.

22

Partly Sunny

For the first year and a half after the divorce, I was so depressed that I couldn't go back out into the fields. When I would go to work at my dad's, I would immediately go into my windowless, cubicle-sized office and immerse myself in bookkeeping for the farm, or managing my dad's personal finances. It was too painful to think about going back out into the fields and starting over on my Almond Timeline, reconstructing what had taken me ten years to put together. The notes in my Almond Timeline were like my textbooks. They recorded the standard work for the fields that my dad had told me about season after season, and how to conduct the farm's operations. They also functioned as a kind of historical archive for my family, and once that archive was gone, it could not be replicated.

Each day, as I worked in the office, my dad would encourage me to get back out into the fields with him and to think about projects I could start, and goals I could set. He tried to reenergize my spirit and remind me of the many things I had to be thankful for. Every Sunday, I would pick up my dad and Charlotte for church in the morning, and that evening, I would bring over dinner and we'd all eat together. The routine of those Sundays helped to suspend some of the mental and physical distress I was experiencing in the aftermath of the divorce.

By spending time with my dad and Charlotte, I also realized that they had a deep spiritual thirst that was drawing them closer to God. They would tell me how much they looked forward to going to church every Sunday, and how the homily uplifted and motivated them throughout the week. In turn, their devotion uplifted me, and I was happy that I finally had family members to go to church with. At the time, I felt broken, and my dad and Charlotte's shared faith and wisdom made me feel loved and wanted, as though I were among friends.

Three months before her eightieth birthday, Charlotte decided to visit her son in Japan. My dad, as well as her good friends, advised her against going, seeing as it was such a long flight and a long way away, but it didn't matter. Charlotte wanted to go. She had the wherewithal, and there was no talking her out of it.

She stayed in Tokyo for nine days, and the night before she was to return, her daughter, Maisie, called me out of the blue. She was crying before she could even speak.

"What is it?" I asked. "Are you okay? What's wrong?"

"My mom died," Maisie burst out.

All that came out of my mouth was, "No, no, what, what?"

It was hard to believe when she told me what had happened. But it had. In Charlotte's hotel room, there was a small step in the entryway and an indoor Zen-type rock formation beside it. The night before Charlotte was to fly back home to my dad's, she had tripped on the small step in the entryway, fallen, and hit her head on the rock formation, and died.

Maisie asked me if I could please tell my dad. The next morning, at 6:00 a.m., three hours before Charlotte was to have landed at SFO, I drove over to my dad's house to tell him that Charlotte had died. On my way to deliver this awful news, I remembered him telling me the story about how his little sister had died. In a strange coincidence, her name had also been Charlotte. When my dad was eight years old, and Charlotte was six, she died suddenly. Charlotte had had appendicitis and was rushed to the hospital, where doctors performed an emergency surgery to remove her appendix. When my grandpa went to pick Charlotte up from the hospital, she started to walk out holding his hand, then slowly let go and fell to the ground. The doctors surmised that she'd had a blood clot during the surgery.

So here I was, seventy-five years later, telling my dad the same thing that his dad had told him when he was a child: that a girl named Charlotte, whom he'd loved dearly, was not coming home. As I continued, my dad became visibly upset. "No, no, what, what," he kept saying, just as I'd said to Charlotte's daughter when she'd told me what had happened. Charlotte had called my dad the day before she left Japan and told him that she'd had a wonderful time visiting her son, but that she was looking forward to coming home. She told my dad she loved him and would see him in two days.

Charlotte's death took us all by surprise. I thought for sure she would live long after my dad passed. She was so healthy and with-it, and sharp as a tack. The live-in caregiver who helped her and my dad had left a couple of days prior to go to the Philippines for a month, so now my dad was alone in the house, except for me helping out and working in the office.

A few days later, talking in the kitchen with my dad, who

was clearly heartbroken, he turned to me and said, "You know, this is like what happened when my little sister died."

"I thought about that the morning I came over to tell you about Charlotte," I said. "And I've thought about it ever since."

"I don't have any spirit left in me to keep going," he said. "I'm done."

After Charlotte's funeral, and for the next few months, I went over to my dad's house every day, as usual, except that now the tables had been turned, and it was me who was doing the encouraging. I urged my dad to go out into the fields and to write down his goals and projects, just as he had urged me in those first few months after the divorce. It was ironic that my dad's tragedy is what helped me, in part, to get over my own. After Liam's ex-wives helped me to detach myself from him, this was the final phase of my healing.

I realized how important it was to get my dad's mind focused on the beauty of the land and the orchards, and to get him back to thinking about the legacy he had created for future generations. It also made me realize even that much more the importance of family. I now understood the saying that blood is thicker than water. I heard once that if a person dies without a will, his or her inheritance will go down like pipes go in plumbing. The closest relative may not always be who you think should be next in line, nevertheless, family blood is family blood. Blood is symbolic and very real. It can mean sacrifice in harsh ways and in good ways. I thought about the importance of blood in the Passover story, when God's spirit passed over the houses marked with blood on the door frames, and spared those first-born and their families. Blood is life-giving.

23

Blue Skies

Looking back, there were four events when I believe God's Holy Spirit intervened and stepped in to save me from my own demise. The first was the moment of insight I had standing at the kitchen sink, toward the end of my marriage to Liam, when my entire perspective shifted in an instant. The second was at the Mormon church, when a voice inside my head, which I believe was God's Holy Spirit, told me to get up and run out of there. The third was when I believe my Guardian Angel placed an invisible shield next to me in Liam's pickup truck, preventing me from clipping the garage door remote to the visor. If not for my inability to put the new remote on the visor, I never would have noticed the stack of papers that were literally sitting right underneath me, pressing up against the backs of my thighs, practically lifting me up off the seat. The last and final intervention was the spiritual enlightenment I received from Mother Bernadette, when I went seeking help after Liam demanded that I send him $25,000.

Through it all, my Guardian Angel helped me to not become bitter, but to become better, to glorify God.

Last fall, when my dad and I drove out to the orchards to do the field checks, I thought about how when Liam left, he took more than just my papers. He also took my self-esteem. Liam had me convinced that I needed him, the farm needed him, and that it couldn't be run without him; he made himself seem indispensable. Furthermore, he made me second-guess my dad's judgment, as well as the judgment of our employees, who had worked on the farm for many years.

At the beginning of our relationship, Liam had made me feel so competent and confident, but by the end, he had me convinced that I was incapable of doing anything without him. When he completed the spray permit test after he'd started working for my dad, for example, he made a big deal of the fact that he'd passed such a difficult test. Shortly after he left, I was required to take the test myself, and because of Liam's braggadocious rhetoric, I was scared that I would fail. But I studied hard, and I passed the test just fine. The power of a pathological relationship had suppressed my rational mind.

What a master manipulator Liam was to have had both me and my dad, at different times, begging him not to leave. In my case, it happened before we were married, when Liam came to visit in Patterson and threatened to leave if I talked to him about dating other women. I begged him not to go. In my dad's case, it happened after Liam and I were married, when he and my dad were out in the fields working, and I was in Washington, D.C. When Liam threatened to quit, my dad begged him to stay, for my sake.

As we drove past a neighbor's alfalfa field, the smell of freshly cut hay wafted in through the rolled-down windows. I looked over at the windrows of hay, which had not yet been put into rectangular bales. Hundreds of big, bright, yellow butterflies flitted about the entire field. It had been quiet up to that point, neither one of us starting a conversation, until my dad broke the silence. He started out by saying, "That fella had you so fooled, I was beside myself watching you. I don't want to say 'I told you so,' but everybody could see it except for you. Under that even-keeled appearance was a liar. I will say this, though, he was one of the best—con men, that is—that I've ever seen. He was good." My shoulders bent forward as I shrank down into the seat. My dad didn't stop there. "Do you know what you put me through?" he went on. Before I could answer, he continued, "Every day I had to fight that knucklehead just to farm my own land."

"I'm sorry," I said, feeling devastated. "And I'm so very sorry I've caused you all this trouble."

Here I had thought I was doing a good thing by bringing Liam on board, but in reality, I had been putting my dad and his livelihood in jeopardy. What hurt the most is that my relationship with Liam had a detrimental effect not only on my life, but also on the lives of those I loved. I had taken Liam's comment about waving a magic wand to heart, and I believed in the fantasy. Now I felt mortified by the truth. I thought about the Russian proverb Ronald Reagan liked to use, "trust but verify." It wasn't in me to become cynical about others' motives, so from there on out, I resolved to trust but verify. I was not going to be snowed again.

Still driving the dirt roads, my dad and I had now reached one of our older almond orchards. With the windows rolled down, I heard a small gust of wind rustle through the tops of the trees, making the leaves look like shimmering silver feathers. My dad broke the silence again. "Do you remember when Grandpa and me put this bridge in?" he asked, as we approached a small bridge over a canal that runs through our property. "I was wondering how old you were," he said. "Look outta the window, would-ja? See some initials over there in the cement?"

I could see some, but I couldn't read them since they were upside down. Seeking a respite from the intensity of our conversation, I readily hopped out of the pickup and looked at the initials. There they were: VB 2/67. I was six years old when my dad and grandpa had built the bridge and poured the cement, during one of the many times I'd been riding around with them.

Now, forty-six years later, as I stood there looking down at my initials and the date, I realized more than ever how much I loved the land. I felt truly blessed. God had assigned me the task of taking care of this special gift. Land cannot be replicated or manufactured. It produces food for people and animals, and creates jobs that have a global impact. From planting to harvesting, to slicing and dicing in canneries, to trucking and shipping, both domestic and overseas, farming generates a plethora of employment opportunities.

I could have lost it all: my family, the land, and my relationship with God. I almost did. I almost lost it to a person who had violated my code of ethics, fabricated his credentials, and whose words meant absolutely nothing. Someone who seemed so polite and educated, and yet, underneath it all, was deceptive and nefarious. During the latter days of our marriage, and on the brink of divorce, Liam had made me feel so bad about my family loyalty. He scorned me as if I were doing something wrong to have chosen my family and inheritance over him. In the end, though, I made the right choice. I chose blood and land.

My dad interrupted my thoughts again. "Come on, let's go. I'd like to check on field number four. I see Arturo over there disking."

I was also realizing that my dear dad, who'd shown me the meaning of unconditional love, was not going to be able to tell me as much in the near future about the crops and farming. I felt a surge of urgency and hope for the future, and no longer felt despondent about the past. From then on, whenever I went out into the fields, I started voraciously taking as many notes as I could.

An old diseased almond orchard needed to be removed, and I decided that I would make my notes and descriptions even better and more detailed than before. I bought a Polaroid camera, and every day, I documented the process of pulling out the old orchard and planting a new one from start to finish, at every stage. I would write down what had been done that day, and how, and the next steps to take.

It's about a two-year wait time from when the baby trees are ordered to when they are delivered for planting. Meanwhile, the old orchard gets pulled out and lots of work must be done to prepare the ground. A soil analysis has to be conducted to evaluate mineral nutrition and fertilization, and then, based on those findings, amendments are made to the soil. There are also decisions to be made, such as which variety of almond trees to plant, and on what type of rootstock. This can depend on a number of factors, including the pollination and cross-pollination, the bloom, and the timing of when the almonds are ready to be harvested. Water is an extremely important factor; choosing an irrigation method can depend on the soil, the climate, and the quality and availability of the water. The spacing of the trees also needs to be configured, because it affects the amount of sunlight that each tree gets as it matures, which can affect its production.

The day finally came when the baby almond trees, both Nonpareil and Aldrich varieties, were delivered. It was a cold winter day in January, as this is the best time for planting. The soil is a rich, dark color, filled with nutrients, and soft and pliable before the ground becomes too frozen for planting. "We have good ground," my grandpa always told me. "It's Hanford loam." My now young adult children, Cody and Hannah, were there that memorable day as we drove out to the barn and watched the trees being planted.

I stood there, looking at hundreds of new trees being carefully placed in the holes at a slight angle toward the north, and their fingerling roots being gently spread out in the soil. Even though the land was my birthright and inheritance, I felt as though everything I had been through with Liam was God's way of making me earn it in my own right. As the great Saint Padre Pio said, "Ask not 'why' we suffer, but ask 'what for' are we suffering." In the past, I had kept asking "why," when trying to find the meaning of my suffering. Now I finally understood, the answer wasn't in the "why," it was in the "what for."

I had to earn it. That was the "what for." That was the meaning of my suffering.

I was so thankful that God had shown me not to take for granted all that He had given me. God had put obstacles in my path, entrusting me with adversity, in order to bring me closer to Him. He gave me the resilience I needed to get through the trials. Like a tree that gets pruned after harvest to make it stronger and bear more fruit the following year, God was pruning me so that I would become stronger. I no longer ask why things happen, instead I ask "what for." By seeing how much someone else wanted what I had, and to what extreme measures they would go to get it, I learned to value my own self-worth, and to never allow one person to have so much control over my soul.

The anticipation of spring's new growth and caring for the baby trees filled me with hope for the future. Time heals. Time repairs. Time nourishes. There is no shortcut to healing a broken heart or to ending suffering, but I have found that if I can press on one day at a time through despairing situations, sure as the tides will ebb and flow, tomorrow will be a new day. And with each new day comes a new beginning.

Resources

- www.saferelationshipsmagazine.com
- www.verbalabuse.com
- www.lovefraud.com
- *The Verbally Abusive Relationship: How to Recognize it and How to Respond* by Patricia Evans
- *How to Spot a Dangerous Man Before You Get Involved* and any books by Sandra L. Brown
- *The Sociopath Next Door* by Martha Stout